MORE
BUSTING
BAD GUYS

True Crime Stories of Cocaine, Cockfights, and Cold-Blooded Killers

MARK LANGAN

MTL 838

OMAHA, NEBRASKA

Paperback ISBN: 978-0-9913110-4-0
Kindle ISBN: 978-0-9913110-5-7
EPUB ISBN: 978-0-9913110-6-4

Library of Congress Cataloging Number: 2020912818

MTL838 LLC
P.O. Box 34653
Omaha, NE 68134

www.BustingBadGuys.com

Designed and produced by Concierge Marketing Inc. and Book Publishing Services.
Printed in the United States of America.
10   9   8   7   6   5   4   3   2

MORE
BUSTING
BAD GUYS

To my dad, Jerry Langan, US Marshal,
who taught me the importance of treating bad guys fairly.

CONTENTS

Part II: From Busting Meth Labs to Chasing Black Labs

JUST WHEN I THOUGHT I'D SEEN IT ALL ...

I cannot count the times I've met someone for the first time and, when they find out I'm a retired narcotics sergeant on the Omaha Police force, they say, "Man, I bet you've seen it all."

Most of the time I respond by saying, "Yeah, I suppose you can say that."

But have I really seen it all? Do cops ever really see it all? I saw some crazy stuff for sure.

I went into houses that were beyond livable. Human and dog feces, maggots, and vermin were a common occurrence. I stopped wondering why people wiped their asses and threw the toilet paper into nearby trash cans because we often found the stash of drugs at the bottom of that pile of shit-stained toilet paper. The stench was unbearable, and flies were everywhere.

We saw mice running around kids' bedrooms. There were houses where I would tap the ceiling with a broom handle only to hear the scatter of mice feet. That always freaked me out.

Many cops I worked with are anally organized, and their houses and yards are meticulous. I fall into that category—and for good reason. I saw the worst living conditions there were.

I experienced firsthand the adrenaline rush of crashing through the front door of a drug house and chasing suspects through hallways and bedrooms before they were able to flush the drugs. Of the many exciting aspects of police work, being the first through the door is hard to compete with.

One time we had just hit a house and had all the suspects secured with handcuffs. Seconds prior it was sheer pandemonium with everybody running and screaming and trying to escape. One of my guys turned to me and in an excited tone said, "Sarge, this is better than sex!" At the time it was hard to argue.

I saw the devastating effects of alcohol. Several times I was at the scene of fatality accidents involving drunk drivers. Innocent kids were killed in mangled messes of vehicles. These images never leave my mind.

I made so many domestic violence calls in my career that I can't even remember them all. Most involved alcohol. Women were beaten, kids were abused, and dogs were kicked by abusive men under the influence of alcohol.

Many times, I encountered a drunk guy who thought he was tougher than he should have been.

"I'm going to kick your ass!" many a drunkard said to me.

"Sir," I would reply, "you are suffering from a bad case of liquor courage. I suggest you shut up unless you want to go to jail."

Most of the time they would settle down, especially when my impressive convoy of backup officers arrived.

I saw firsthand the best and worst of human beings.

Methamphetamine is a bad drug, and so many users that I encountered let the drug ruin their lives. There was no coming back for them. Sadly, their bodies and brains withered away. They destroyed any family relationships they had. Kids were the innocent victims, and many gravitated into the early use of marijuana and alcohol, leading to worse drugs such as meth and fentanyl.

I saw countless lives ruined through the use of drugs and alcohol. Many ended up prison, and many more died from years of abuse. But I also knew those who rose from the ashes and turned their negative lifestyle into a positive force for themselves and those near and dear.

I can honestly say that people can change. I have met so many people I previously arrested who have now seen the light. Some were interviewed for this book.

I personally know past drug dealers who have new lives in unique areas such as horticulture (no, not growing pot!), drug counseling, managing restaurants, and selling cars. One is a major player in an Omaha nonprofit organization for the poor and disenfranchised. Others are simply raising their kids, like most parents do.

Over the years I think I have been unfairly characterized by some close to me, and others not so close to me, as being hard core and callous when it comes to giving second chances. Believe me when I say I know people can change, and I enjoy seeing the results.

Just when I thought I had seen it all, I arrested the PTA mom from small-town Nebraska who was prostituting herself over the internet. Or the time I found a couple having sex in plain sight in a city park only to find out the young lady was getting married in two days—and she was having sex with the best man.

And when we found a little guy having anal sex with a 300-pound prostitute in the cab of his semi at a truck-stop parking lot. My partner said it looked like a Chihuahua fucking a St. Bernard. By the way, he was not wearing a condom.

I received a radio call of a woman handcuffed to a bedpost, and the key was not working to unlock her. I raced to the scene to find a young lady at her boyfriend's house. They wanted to spice things up a bit, so he brought out an old pair of handcuffs.

When I arrived, she was naked under a blanket that he was carefully holding in place. Both of her wrists were cuffed to the headboard. The word *embarrassed* does not do justice. Perhaps *mortified* describes it best. Luckily, my key worked, and I was able to release her. I promise I didn't peek (at least not too much).

Then there was the teenage son who was pimping his mother out. I could go on and on.

I encountered so much death while I was a cop—during my years as a rookie, a beat cop, an undercover vice cop, and as a narcotics sergeant before I retired in 2004.

Shooting victims do not look like they are portrayed on television. Splattered brain matter is common in head shots. For those stabbed in the gut, we'd often see intestines hanging out of their stomach.

Sudden infant death syndrome cases were the toughest. Seeing a little angel lying lifeless in a crib is tough to handle. I always felt bad for the parents who made the discovery.

Old people who died in their sleep were not so tough. We were required to make the calls just to ensure nothing fishy had occurred. Most had lived good lives and simply drifted off to heaven during the night. I was always impressed by the outpouring of family support that would gather at these homes.

I've interviewed so many young gang members who had the mindset that they would not live past the age of twenty-one. Therefore, they were going to cause as much havoc as possible. Imagine being a parent and knowing that your child, whom you love more than life itself, plans on being killed by a rival gang before they even have a chance to live life as an adult.

Of course, most of these young impressionable gang members had no parental support growing up. Hence their negative attitude toward life.

But, I encountered many mamas over the years who raised sons in gang-infested areas of Omaha and were able to provide guidance and leadership. They taught the tough-love concept—meaning their sons had best not do anything to disappoint Mama.

Just imagine how scary it was to hear gunshots nightly outside your house, knowing your teenage son would soon be walking home from his job. Or how tough it was to keep the allure of fast money, and faster women, from overtaking your son. I have a huge respect for these mothers, most of whom had no husband in the picture, for providing a foundation for these boys to build their lives on. Many became fine Omaha Police officers who went back to patrol the neighborhoods they grew up in.

I have attended three funerals for Omaha Police officers killed in the line of duty. The negative effects of a line-of-duty death weigh heavily on the troops. We always wonder that the deceased could have been us. And those close to the slain officer think why couldn't it have been me.

Yes, I have certainly seen a lot. And my experiences have taken a toll. How could they not?

MORE BUSTING BAD GUYS

Since the publication of my first book, *Busting Bad Guys: My True Crime Stories of Bookies, Drug Dealers, and Ladies of the Night* in 2014, I have done over 250 book signings and promotional events.

Most happenings have been in my hometown of Omaha, Nebraska, where the book has developed almost a cult-like following. I am amazed at the number of people I have previously arrested who approach me in restaurants, bars, and book-signing events.

Many ask, "Am I in your book?" or "Please tell me I am not in your book!"

Most have been cordial, considering the fact that I put many of them in prison—well, they put themselves there.

Several years ago I walked into my favorite spot, Leo's Diner, in the revitalized boho Benson area of midtown Omaha. A large intimidating man was sitting in a booth facing the door. As soon as our eyes met, I realized he knew me, and probably not for the right reasons. If looks could kill, I would have fallen over dead right there into a plate of Leo's famous hangover breakfast.

His eyes stayed on me as I walked by and took a stool at the counter near the cash register. I frequently glanced over my shoulder, making sure the guy didn't have any ill-conceived notions.

After several minutes Roxi the waitress whispered in my ear, "See the guy in the front booth? He says he knows you."

I told Roxi I wasn't surprised, given the icy stare when I walked in.

"He wants to talk to you," she said.

I cautiously walked up to the table and, surprisingly, he extended his hand to mine. I was immediately at ease with his smile and calm demeanor. My initial impression of him was wrong, which is probably all too common when a burly African American guy stares at a white guy like me.

I misjudged that situation.

"Mark," he said, "you probably don't remember me, but back in the early eighties I was standing on the corner of 24th and Sprague around ten at night. I was drunk and taking a leak on the sidewalk when you raced up in your police car and caught me midstream."

I had no idea where this story was going, but it was holding my interest for sure. After all, he was recounting something from over thirty years ago.

"Instead of arresting me, you decided to read me the riot act. Mark, you told me this neighborhood belonged to you, and what I was doing was not allowed. I'll never forget it, man. You scared me to death. You coulda arrested me and you didn't. I've never forgotten that and want to thank you."

With that we shook hands, and he surprised me by saying, "And I want to buy two of your books!"

On another occasion, I was shopping in a grocery store. A guy who was employed at the store stopped me as I walked by him. He proceeded to tell me how I arrested him for selling methamphetamine around twenty years ago. He gave me the address where I snagged him, the time of year, and even mentioned that the raid happened around midnight. He seemed a bit offended that I didn't remember that time when we splintered his front door with a battering ram and changed his life forever.

I did hundreds such raids over the years and could not remember each one. For twenty-six years, I worked the night shift, keeping Omaha safe from the bad guys while my family (and yours) slept.

He did a ten-year prison stint and now, at the age of forty-something, was stocking shelves at a grocery store. It's tough for ex-cons to get back on their feet, even years after they screw up their lives.

Then he said, "You know what I remember about that night?"

"I have no idea."

"You let me smoke one last cigarette before you took me to jail. Thanks, man."

With that he shook my hand and went back to work. It's the little luxuries in life that mean so much.

I felt the presence of my father, the career federal lawman, and the man I dedicated this book to. My dad was the Chief Deputy United States Marshal for the District of Nebraska. I loved my dad's stories of handling dangerous prisoners accused of bank robberies, kidnapping, and other violent crimes.

Dad would tell these prisoners that he would treat them with the same respect that he expected in return, but that no rules would be broken. He told me numerous times that the best way he knew to keep a prisoner calm and cooperative was simple: Let them sneak a smoke when they least expected it.

I guess I listened to him more than I ever realized.

When *Busting Bad Guys* was published, my wife and I hosted a book launch event at the Nebraska Humane Society where I was employed at the time as the Vice President of Field Operations. Annette and I were worried nobody would show up to eat the food we had bought.

My dad, Jerry Langan, leading bank robbers outside the federal courthouse in Omaha, Nebraska, July 11, 1971. (Reprinted with permission of the Omaha World-Herald.*)*

Instead, 400 people attended and bought my book. It was a great night, and an even better way to start my new journey as an author. Over the six years since, I have done book-signing events in Seattle, Phoenix, Denver, San Francisco, Atlanta, and Baltimore, to name a few. The support for my story was overwhelming.

Like any cop, I have more stories to tell, and so do my fellow officers. We all have the cases that stick with us. The bad guys who did unspeakable horrors to fellow human beings. The tragedies that still wake us up at night.

This second book, *More Busting Bad Guys*, recounts more of my stories and some of the stories of my fellow officers in blue.

I frequently tell readers of the respect I have for fiction writers. But I have one advantage over those writers. I don't have to make these stories up: running with the Hells Angels, animal sacrifices, that first hit of meth or crack, gangs with strangleholds on neighborhoods, police snipers taking risky shots only inches from innocent victims, or even how my own mother was integral in taking down the biggest crack cocaine operation in Omaha.

Some stories involve no crimes at all, yet they left an impression with me that I have not been able to shake, even forty years later.

Truth is indeed stranger than fiction.

I can still remember the rush I felt before I started my patrol shift from North Assembly at 48th and Ames Avenue.

In that vein, buckle yourself in.

Flip on the lights and siren.

Ride with me as I patrol your streets.

C SHIFT: WHAT HAPPENS FROM FOUR TO MIDNIGHT

1

WHEN DEATH CALLS

Okay, class," Sergeant Hauger began. "I'm going to make this nice and easy. Here's what you do. You walk up to the front door and knock. You stand very tall and confidently, prepared to deliver the bad news.

"The wife answers the door and you immediately state, 'Good afternoon, I'm Sergeant Hauger with the Omaha Police Department. Are you the widow Brown?'

"The wife will say, 'Well, no, I'm not the widow Brown.'

"You respond, 'Well, you are now!'"

The sergeant then finished by telling our training class at the police academy, "You have now officially delivered the death notification, and you can leave and go back into service."

There was an awkward pause, followed by stifled laughter.

To most readers this is probably not funny. I agree that Sergeant Hauger's joke required a certain warped sense of humor in order to appreciate the punchline. But the fact I still remember it over forty years later shows that his lighthearted approach to the sometimes painful parts of police work had a lasting impact.

On August 7, 1978, I began my police academy training with the Omaha Police Department. I was a starry-eyed nineteen-year-old kid who had to grow up rapidly so I could deal with what awaited me on the streets.

One advantage I had was I realized in my heart how quickly I needed to mature. I took my academy training seriously and idolized the instructors. These were guys who had already proven themselves on the streets of Omaha. They were hand-picked for the coveted position of an academy instructor and were meant to instill their vast knowledge in us green rookies.

Officers like Doug Irvin and Dave Schlotman wore crisp uniforms to work each day and always had their police hats perfectly in place whenever they left Central Police Headquarters. They regaled the class with war stories about domestic violence calls or dead bodies they found decomposing, half-eaten by the dog left to starve after the owner died while watching television in an easy chair.

I remember wondering if there was any chance I would someday be like them. I admit I had my doubts.

Sgt. Vern Hauger was the favorite instructor among many of us recruits. He had a great sense of humor and was constantly slipping in one-liners that caused us to laugh. The Sarge was the first to teach me that cops had a calloused sense of humor acquired over years on the streets seeing and smelling horrendous things they were forced to deal with.

I learned that cops' humor is most likely not funny to the average citizen. In fact, many would be offended by it. But as I've said many times, cops are different than most people, and we certainly speak our own language.

Sadly, police officers are often the bearer of bad news about the loss of a loved one. Whether someone was the victim of a homicide, car accident, or of simply dropping dead of a heart attack while taking a walk, it's never good to have a police officer knock on your door.

Sergeant Hauger walked confidently into the recruit class as the session began. I had pen in hand, since we were required to take extensive notes and then go home that night and type them out (on my manual typewriter) to be placed in a three-ring notebook that we were graded on weekly.

I was planning to be well prepared on the streets to deliver the terrible news about the loss of a loved one.

After telling us the joke about the widow Brown, the Sarge then became serious and told us how important our training was on death notification calls. We needed to be professional, calm, and to the point.

He told us that the last thing a police officer should do is hem and haw with the other person we were dealing with. Deliver the news and make sure the other person is taken care of before we leave.

And the last talking point Sergeant Hauger had for us was this: "Do not show emotion yourself. Be compassionate, yet do not break down. The police officer needs to be a solid presence in the room during this difficult time."

Fast-forward six months and I was assigned to a one-officer cruiser in the north central area of town. My assigned district was four square miles of suburban middle-class houses, low-income apartments, lots of retail outlets, and Immanuel Hospital.

My calls ranged from burglaries to robberies, domestic violence to missing juveniles, shopliftings to stolen cars, and the obligatory calls every night to the hospital's emergency room for assaults and vehicle injury accidents.

Around 6:00 p.m. in the spring of 1979 the dispatcher called me on the radio and told me to call the captain's office. This was never a good thing. It seemed the only time I was directed to call the captain was when a citizen was complaining about how I handled a call or accusing me of driving too fast through a neighborhood.

I immediately proceeded to call the captain's office in the way we made phone calls in 1979. I went to the nearest drive-up payphone and nervously dropped a dime.

This call was different than others I had made previously. The captain's tone of voice was serious. He gave me an address and told me to deliver a message to the residents that their daughter had been killed in a car accident in Massachusetts.

The captain supplied me the name and phone number of the law enforcement agency handling the terrible situation in Massachusetts.

My heart began skipping as I realized the gravity of this situation. Here I was, a brand-new rookie, about to tell a parent of their child's demise.

I pulled in front of the house and took a breath. I remembered Sergeant Hauger's instructions on staying professional and having a calm, reassuring demeanor.

I climbed the cement steps next to the driveway, which led to a small sidewalk in front of the picture window of the house. Next, there were three more steps leading to the front door. With each step I became more nervous.

Normally cops bang loudly on doors when they are looking for wanted parties, or bang on a door with their wooden nightsticks, trying to override the loud music that is keeping the neighbors up at night. I chose a normal knock, almost hoping nobody was home.

The door was answered by a middle-aged woman who appeared shocked and concerned about the uniformed police officer standing on her porch.

"Ma'am, I'm Officer Langan with the Omaha Police Department. May I step in and talk to you?"

She appeared hesitant but opened the door.

"What is going on?" she asked cautiously, as I began stepping into her living room.

"Ma'am, if you don't mind, I'd prefer to talk to you inside the house."

As soon as I was in the living room, I noticed a montage of framed pictures on the living room wall. They were all of the same young lady, spanning from infancy to grade school, high school to college, and now as an adult living in Massachusetts.

It was the woman's only child.

She was growing concerned as the seconds passed, and I remembered the sergeant's words, "Do not hem and haw around. Tell them the news right away."

"Ma'am, is there anybody in the house?"

This is a common police question for officer safety aspects, but in this situation, I was asking for support for both me and this poor woman. She said she was a widow and lived alone, which only added to the weight on my shoulders.

"Please, sit down," I said as I gestured to her sofa.

Without hesitating I said the fatal words she would hear forever replaying in her mind: "Ma'am, I have terrible news. Your daughter was involved in a vehicle accident in Massachusetts. I'm so sorry to say she did not survive."

The weight was off my shoulders. I exhaled a huge breath and now braced for this mother's reaction.

She was shocked and had me repeat my words several times.

"This is not happening. This is not happening," she said over and over.

I stayed with her until some family members arrived. This was the least I could do, as she became more distraught as the minutes passed.

After leaving, I recall driving to a nearby parking lot and decompressing from this stressful assignment. I admit I was shaken up. I knew I would never forget this day.

Before I wrote this chapter, I drove by the house, forty-one years after I first knocked on that door. I counted the cement steps leading to the front door. I looked at the picture window I stood in front of, and from my car I peered into the living room where the daughter's photographs had hung and where I delivered the news.

I couldn't help but wonder where life had taken this mother. Did she recover emotionally? Where is the daughter buried? What became of those framed pictures?

I then pulled away from the house and drove straight to the same parking lot from 1979. I again found myself taking a few deep breaths and wondering about the mysteries of life and how quickly it can be taken away.

Then, while parked in the same spot from over forty years ago, I began writing this story.

In 2012 my beloved training sergeant Vern Hauger wrote a book titled *On the Job: An Omaha Police Officer's Story 1958–1988.*

It is a fascinating read about Vern's exploits on the streets of Omaha. Vern wrote, "I have experienced things only a few people will experience. I have been places and seen things that I would never have been able to do if I had not been a police officer. I have rubbed shoulders with people from all walks of life and discovered there is good in the worst of people and there is bad in the best of people."

One of Vern's stories involves a circus lion loose in downtown Omaha. That's a hard one to top for an author like myself (don't worry, the lion was safely captured).

Prior to Vern's book being published, he called me and asked that I write the Foreword. It was a true honor to write about my full circle relationship with Sergeant Hauger, from the youngest recruit officer in class 1-1978 to now, writing an important chapter in the story of his life as a cop.

Sgt. Vern Hauger died in 2014, and at his memorial service his wife asked that I read the Foreword I had written for his book.

Vern was one of a kind.

2

SNIPER: TWENTY-FOUR HOURS OF TERROR

O fficers Randy Eddy and Greg Stanzel were both SWAT-trained Omaha Police officers. They had no idea when they woke up on a chilly December morning four days after Christmas in 1988 how important their training would become. They were called upon, and pressured by their superiors, to make the ultimate split-second decision that would result in either the rescue of a hostage or a complete catastrophic failure that neither officer could have rebounded from.

Cops do not consider taking a life lightly.

Over the years, certain true crime stories have resonated with me. Most are situations that I know about firsthand, based on my own experiences.

In my first book, I dealt with cases I was comfortable writing about. I lived them and loved them enough to share these cherished stories with my readers.

The vivid details still resonate with me, over forty years later. They were easy for me to write.

In this book I am branching out a bit by trying to capture the specific life-changing details of a case that I had nothing to do with. Yet I have always found the circumstances, and the violent resolution, to be extremely impactful.

For the fans of the television show *Blue Bloods*, believe me when I say that Detective Danny Reagan's penchant for shooting and killing multiple suspects and then, in the next scene, sitting with his family at Sunday dinner as if nothing happened is Hollywood fantasy.

For the record, I am a big fan of *Blue Bloods*.

I decided early on as I began to write this chapter to research police reports and media stories and interview those involved to best document for you, the reader, the heart and soul of real-life street stories.

I sat down with the police officers directly involved, as well as a couple of the hostages held during this siege. I enjoyed recording interviews with Officers Eddy and Stanzel. It was amazing to hear and see their emotions as they recounted their actions, over thirty years later.

As I said, traumatic incidents never leave an officer's mind or soul.

The hostages I talked to are still scarred by the incident. As the story progresses, you will hear from them about the everlasting effects of a madman repeatedly pointing a gun at them. One hostage still has vivid memories of being zip-tied to a suitcase containing a functional bomb. One hostage provided me with her poignant handwritten notes from that ordeal.

Yes, all this occurred in Omaha, Nebraska, on December 29 and 30, 1988.

Omaha Police Officer Randy Eddy, a sniper, lay prone on the cold driveway exactly 110 feet from the left eye socket of the hostage-taker's head. The bad guy was clutching the female hostage from behind while holding a handgun to her head. The hostage's head was a mere six inches from the "kill spot."

Unbeknownst to Officer Eddy, another police officer was standing eight inches to the right of where the .308-caliber bullet would travel at 2,800 feet per second. Officer Eddy had less than a second to make his decision to shoot.

THE BAD GUY

Michael Fane was a twenty-one-year-old drifter with mental health issues. Living in Des Moines, Iowa, with his family, he frequently wandered the 120 miles from his home to Omaha, Nebraska. It was never determined why he liked coming to Omaha, but his choice to do so on December 29, 1988, would ultimately result in twenty-four hours of terror.

A month earlier, Fane had been found mumbling and incoherent at a fast-food store in Sarpy County, Nebraska, located on the south side of Omaha. He was placed in a protective care status and released several days later after mental health officials determined he was not a danger to himself or others.

Family members described Michael Fane as a quiet and sensitive child who had grown into a reclusive, withdrawn young adult. Friends knew him as a bright and regular member of the Mason City (Iowa) High School class of 1985.

However, things changed when Fane enrolled at the University of Iowa in the fall of 1985. He was delving into the world of drugs, including hallucinogens such as LSD. He was obsessed with the Grateful Dead rock band.

"The Grateful Dead is not some innocuous rock group," Fane's father said later in an *Omaha World-Herald* interview. "They are a cult, like the Satanism bands."

His father told of his son telling him about taking 100 hits of LSD at a Grateful Dead concert in Atlanta. He said, "Michael was never the same again."

After his committal in Sarpy County, Fane returned to his family in Des Moines and immediately began making threats.

"I need to blow something up," his grandmother reported later as overhearing Fane to say. The grandmother, nor fellow family members, did not notify authorities about Fane's threat.

Instead, on December 29, 1988, Fane stole his grandmother's car and drove westbound on Interstate 80 to Omaha. His plan was simple:

He wanted to commandeer a store, take hostages, and make demands for supplies that would allow to him to build a time machine. The location he picked needed to be near a cemetery, which he would visit, for no particular reason, prior to hijacking the yet-to-be-determined business.

In a matter of hours lives would be changed forever. This included the lives of an Omaha Police Department sniper and his trusted spotter, both of whom would be called upon to make the most impactful and difficult decision of their young lives.

"I'M TAKING OVER"

Darla, one of the beauty operators, wrote her recollections of the events. She had happy Christmas memories just days earlier with her parents and family, including her sons. She hadn't wanted to go to work that Thursday, but she had a busy schedule. A "no show" haircut allowed her to take an earlier lunch break around 2:30 with her family.

Her handwritten notes that she shared with me said she returned to the salon around 3:00 p.m., just as the boss and her daughter were leaving on break.

She wrote, "There was just a feeling I can't describe. But I went on back knowing I had a perm due in about 3:30. ... As I walked from the back of the salon to my station, I noticed a young guy approaching the front door. (I'm pretty confident still that I was the first to see Michael Fane come in.) This did not look like one of our regular customers, and what was peculiar to me right away was the fact he was carrying a sack with something in it in front of him as he walked in.

"Stepping inside the door of the salon, he pointed a gun in the air and said, 'I'm taking over!'"

THE TERROR BEGINS

On Thursday, December 29, 1988, around 3:00 p.m., the calls poured into the Douglas County 911 Center in Omaha.

911: Emergency Service.

Caller: Yeah, we'd like to have a cruiser down here at 6519 Sunshine Drive. We've got a gunman over here in the beauty shop. He's got hostages.

Second Caller: I was getting my hair cut at Possibilities Hair Salon and this guy came in with a gun and said he's taking over. He says he wants us to call the police and he'll give you the response of what he needs.

Within minutes Fane was in contact with 911 and began his irrational demands:

911: Emergency Services.

Fane: Is this the police?

911: Yes, it is.

Fane: I'm down here at Possibilities Hair Salon, and I'm holding hostages. With a gun.

911: What's your name?

Fane: My name is unimportant.

911: Okay, what do you want?

Fane: I'm going to make some demands. For starters, you can start rounding up twelve three-quarter-inch carriage head bolts that are twelve inches long. And you know that type of epoxy putty that you use to repair gas tanks and in plumbing repairs?

911: Yeah.

Fane: I want enough to fill three cubic feet. I want two three-by-three-foot sheets of plexiglass, and an X-Acto knife, and that will be it for now. I hope you realize that this hair salon is an old bank. It has bulletproof glass.

911: What are you going to do with this stuff?

Fane: That is unimportant. I'm also going to need a hacksaw and torch.

Then, the conversation turned to how these supplies would be delivered to Fane inside of the hair salon:

Fane: There's a glass foyer that's in the front that is the entrance to the building. When you come to deliver the supplies, there will be one man, unarmed, and he will carry everything up and place it in the foyer. I will be covering one of the hostages throughout the time.

911: Is there a particular reason you picked this business?

Fane: Yes, as a matter of fact. God showed me the way.

By 4:30 p.m., over an hour after Fane had taken the hostages, the Possibilities Hair Salon was surrounded by members of the Omaha Police Department SWAT team, known as the Emergency Response Unit. The ERU was a group of highly trained officers who specialized in high-risk search warrants and barricaded gunmen situations.

However, for most of these officers, this was the first hostage situation they had encountered.

Two different snipers were positioned across the street to see the front of the hair salon. Other officers took strategic spots around all four corners of the building.

Soon the area was in total lockdown. The negotiations began.

THE HOSTAGES

Laura Nalley was hung over after attending a concert the night before. She was a hair stylist in the Possibilities Hair Salon, and she was waiting for her last appointment so she could go home and crash.

I interviewed her in 2016.

"Sharma [a fellow stylist] and I were watching Oprah on TV and she kind of turned white. She said, 'He's got a gun!'"

Michael Fane had strolled through the front door of Possibilities Hair Salon armed with a handgun and immediately began making demands.

"He told us to get on the floor," Laura recalled, "which of course we did. The gal next to me kept talking and he didn't like that. He said, 'Who is talking, who is talking?' Fane started screaming, 'This is my place, I'm taking it, I'm taking it!'"

Laura was confused, as she initially assumed Fane had come to the shop to rob it. It was quickly apparent that this was not Fane's intention, and that's when things became scary.

"Me being Catholic, I started praying the rosary," she said.

Laura was twenty-nine and in top shape. The slender redhead, wearing the popular 1980s large glasses, had recently taken up running through her South Omaha neighborhood. "Jogging was my chance to clear my mind," she later recalled.

She was single and had lost her mother when she was nineteen. She was close with her father, whom she still lived with five minutes from the hair salon.

When Fane entered the store, he was wearing his long dark hair in a ponytail bound by a red rubber band. He was 6 foot 2 and skinny, weighing 160 pounds. He also had a full beard and mustache.

Fane was wearing a green army-type coat when he walked in. Under the coat he had on a gray long-sleeved V-neck shirt and medium blue cloth trousers held up by blue suspenders. He was wearing tannish hiking boots with red shoestrings and white socks.

Fane was holding eight hostages. Five women, including Laura, were employees. The others were either customers or those who were waiting for someone to get their hair cut. One hostage included a five-year-old boy.

"I was pretty sure we were all done at that point," Laura said. "We were upside down on the floor in a big circle. I kept thinking, isn't he just going to take the money? Isn't someone just going to open the cash drawer for him? All of a sudden he came over and poked me and told me to get up."

She continued, "And I said, 'Why, am I leaving?' He had the pistol next to my head and he walked me over to the phone. He told me to call 911.

"When I picked up the phone, it was already connected to 911, and they said, 'What's going on there?' And I said, 'He wants to talk to you people.'"

After the calls to 911 Laura was told by Fane that she and another hostage would be leaving the store. It was her impression that there were too many hostages for Fane to handle, and he wanted to reduce the numbers so he could be more in control of the situation.

"He walked us to the door," she remembered, "and he had the gun at my head. He says, 'I need you to leave. I need you to go get the police.'"

Laura was unaware that, by this time, the Omaha Police Department had secured that entire area. There was no foot or vehicle traffic allowed, and police officers were posted inconspicuously around the hair salon.

"And I ran out that door. It was really eerie. There was nobody around, there was no traffic."

Fane also released three other hostages, including the five-year-old boy.

Laura ran to a nearby bar where the Omaha Police had set up a command post. She had been held hostage for twenty minutes.

The police officers immediately had Laura draw maps of the interior of the salon and also provide a good description of Fane and how he was acting.

To me, she described her time as a hostage as sobering. "I was under control. I was going to stay alert, and I wanted to know what I had to do to get out of there."

Several of the female hostages could not stop crying while lying on the floor. She described them as sobbing, shaking, and blubbering. Laura recalled Fane as saying he wanted to build a "ship to God or something."

Thirty years later Laura still has flashbacks about being taken hostage and having a gun put to her head: "If everyone had a gun in the head once in their life, they would love the rest of their life."

During my interview with Laura it was apparent she took pride in the strength she showed that day, under dangerous circumstances.

She said, "I did not cry. I felt an inner peace with God that he would get me through it. I felt if I died that day, I was okay."

DANGER COMES TO THE NEIGHBORHOOD

Possibilities Hair Salon was located in a small, unique business district in South Omaha. The building previously housed a bank. The one-story structure with the two-tone brown color scheme was constructed with one set of narrow windows measuring twenty inches wide and five feet tall on all sides of the building. It was difficult to catch glimpses of Fane due to the narrow windows.

The front entrance was also narrow, not more than five feet wide with a double set of full glass doors, first leading into an alcove, and then into the business. The drive-through portion of the old bank still existed with the overhang covering that portion of the parking lot.

As customers entered the south main doors, they were greeted by a welcome desk and receptionist area to their left. The main business area was behind the receptionist desk, with a spacious area for the stylists to work in. This would be the main area where Fane held his hostages.

Toward the east end of the hair salon were two bathrooms, hair washing stations, an office, and an electrical room. The only other exit was a back door on the east side of the building near the bathrooms.

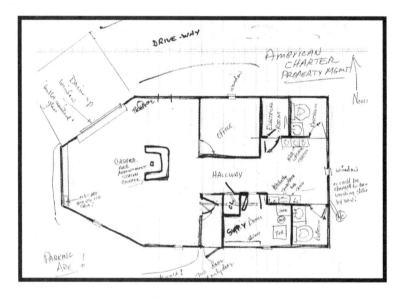

This diagram, drawn with the help of released hostages, is the interior of the Possibilities Hair Salon.

At one time home to the largest stockyards in the world, South Omaha was, and continues to be, culturally diverse. Many residents are descended from the Czech, Irish, Italian, Latino, Lithuanian, and Polish immigrants who made up the original workforce in the meatpacking industry. These immigrants were primarily Roman Catholic.

One of the best allures of South Omaha were small pockets of family-run businesses nestled in the middle of working-class neighborhoods.

This area was no different. To the east of the hair salon was the popular Darby's Tavern, a brisk one-story Irish-themed watering hole surrounded by small, one-story houses.

To the southwest of the hair salon was Veys Foodland, owned by former Omaha Mayor Al Veys. The business had long been a staple of this neighborhood.

This was one of many South Omaha neighborhoods where one could walk a block or two to buy groceries, get a haircut, or drink a cold one.

The area was now totally locked down by police. SWAT personnel were in place. Command officers had taken over Darby's Tavern to use as a command post.

The media were swarming the area and were warned several times not to broadcast the positioning of the Emergency Response Unit (SWAT) personnel. ERU command officers were aware that Fane was watching a television set inside the hair salon.

Omaha Police took over Darby's Tavern as a command post during the hostage situation in the hair salon nearby.

One police officer was able to gain a vantage point to see into the salon. The officer plainly saw a semiautomatic handgun in Fane's hand. It appeared to the officer that Fane was allowing the remaining four female hostages to use the restroom.

At 5:20 p.m. an ERU sergeant reported seeing three female hostages face down on the floor. The fourth hostage could not be seen but was later determined to still be safe.

BORN TO BE A SNIPER

Omaha Police Officer Randy Eddy was born to be a sniper. His grandfather was a World War I veteran whom he grew to idolize. He enjoyed remembering his grandfather when I interviewed him in 2016.

"He was absolutely one hell of a rifle shooter. The man could shoot pheasants and quail out of the air with a .22 rifle."

Out of high school Eddy went into the Marines and quickly excelled. "I went in as an anti-tank gunner. I was taught how to blow up Russian tanks." He was one of two Marines selected out of 600 to be assigned to Washington, DC, for security duties.

"After my first year, a captain says, 'Hey, I was looking at your scores in boot camp and you did very well with a rifle.' He asked me, 'How would you like to shoot on the Marine Corp rifle and pistol team?'"

For the next two years Eddy excelled at his shooting competitions. He was especially competent with his rifle. In fact, he became a rifle instructor. He left the Marines and joined the Omaha Police Department in 1981.

"It was an easy transition for me. I tried out for the ERU and I made it," he told me.

Seven years later found Eddy lying on a cold cement driveway, under a parked van, with a clear view of the front door of Possibilities Hair Salon. He was armed with a Remington 700 police special rifle, made to fire a .308-caliber round.

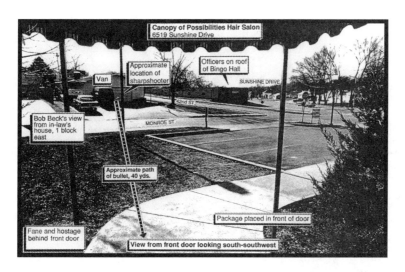

Schematic diagram documenting the perimeter around the Possibilities Hair Salon. (Reprinted with permission of the Omaha World-Herald.*)*

The rifle was equipped with a Leopold 6.5 x 20 scope, allowing Eddy to see what color eyes the suspect had. His training would soon be put to the test.

But Randy Eddy had a problem. As the sniper, it was his responsibility to ensure that if he took a shot, it would hit the intended target.

Michael Fane had picked a challenging location to take hostages. Prior to becoming Possibilities Hair Salon, the building was a bank. In fact, it was constructed to be a bank, meaning the windows were extra thick and, in some locations, double-paned. There was confusion as to whether the windows were actually bulletproof.

Police officers scrambled to interview an original owner of the building that housed the salon. They learned that all the windows were, in fact, bulletproof except for the main door glass that faced to the south.

At a certain point into the hostage standoff, the snipers, including Randy Eddy, were told to take a shot on Fane if the situation presented itself. Fane was making outlandish demands that he was on a mission from God to build a time machine.

IS A BOMB INSIDE THE RED SUITCASE?

Fane upped the ante soon after taking his hostages inside the hair salon. He had brought in a red nylon suitcase with yellow trim. He was consistently seen pointing a handgun at the heads of hostages and continued bragging to police negotiators that he had a bomb in the red suitcase.

Negotiations were up and down with Fane. His moods would change from talkative to threatening, and the chatter among him and the negotiators was breaking down at certain points about releasing more hostages.

At 5:55 p.m., close to three hours into the ordeal, Officer Eddy advised ERU command located in Darby's Tavern that because of the double-paned glass of the main doors, he would not be able to shoot unless the suspect was outside.

Spotter Greg Stanzel, far left, standing next to sniper Randy Eddy during the hostage incident at the command post outside Darby's Tavern.

Eddy recalls being pressured by his command officers to shoot the suspect through the bank's windows if the opportunity presented itself.

He said to me, "There was a side window, but it was double-paned bulletproof glass. He [Fane] was exposed all by himself. Take him through the glass, I was told. My concern was if the bullet hit the glass, it was going to shatter. Now we've got a bullet traveling 2,800 feet per second, hitting the glass ... the bullet might fragment and not take the suspect down, enabling him to possibly detonate the bomb."

To clarify, I asked Eddy, "But you were told to take a shot through the window, and you said, I'm not going to do it."

"That's right," he said. "Taking him through the side window was a low percentage shot that would risk the lives of the hostages and police officers outside the building."

"The sniper has the final say, I would think," I said.

To which Eddy replied, "It was my ass."

NOT LIKE ON TV

Hostage situations unfold quickly on TV. Not so much in real time when lunatics have guns and bombs.

It was apparent that Fane was mentally unhinged and armed with both. The hostage negotiators and command officers from the ERU were pleased that he had initially released four hostages, including the little boy.

But he still had four hostages under his control, and as the day and night wore on, his demands became more bizarre and worrisome.

Around dinnertime, Fane asked for pizza, some mild tranquilizers, and a quarter ounce of marijuana. The pizza was easy to get, but there was no way the command officers at the scene were going to deliver illegal drugs to Fane. First, that would be illegal and unethical. And most importantly, the drugs could cause increased violent behavior on Fane's part.

Food deliveries were always done the same. A group of ERU officers would carefully approach the front door. Fane, with his gun to the head of hostage, would carefully walk to the door, open it, and have the hostage bend over to pick up food and take it back inside.

Sniper Randy Eddy took note during each delivery as to Fane's body posture relative to when the hostage bent over to pick up the food.

"I began realizing that by putting the sack out there another two or three feet, the hostage had to reach a little bit further. That would give me another second or two—"

An extra second is a lot of time for a sniper to make a life-or-death decision.

A HOSTAGE REMEMBERS THE FEAR

Denise was one of the original hostages taken by Michael Fane. She was quiet and reclusive when I interviewed her in 2016. I felt bad at certain points during my time with her, since it seemed like I was reopening old wounds.

She and her five-year-old son had gone with her boyfriend to the Possibilities Hair Salon so the boyfriend could get his hair cut. She said, "He was in the middle of his haircut when Michael Fane walked in and said, 'I'm taking this place over.' He had a gun. Then he ordered all of us to get face down on the floor. I remember I had my son lying right next to me. That was my main focus at that time."

Within minutes Fane started releasing hostages, including Denise's boyfriend and son.

"It was just like some pressure off of me to know that my son was leaving the building," she said.

Fane had told the remaining four hostages that besides his gun he had a bomb in the red suitcase he brought into the shop. To make matters worse, Fane produced several plastic zip ties and ordered Denise and another hostage, Darla, to tie themselves to the red suitcase containing the bomb.

"So we reluctantly zip-tied our wrists to the bomb."

After about two hours Fane cut them free from the suitcase, which was a relief for the hostages. But Fane still appeared unstable to Denise, and she was in constant fear for her life.

As she said to me, "One of the reasons he told us that he was taking over the hair salon was that is used to be a bank, and he said it had bulletproof glass. He thought he would have protection."

Denise recalls Fane saying that his mission was to make a time warp machine, which was the reason he was asking for the construction supplies from the police negotiator.

"That wasn't good," Denise told me.

Denise felt that her life may be over at the hands of Michael Fane.

"I was thinking that I probably wasn't going to get out of that situation," she said. "I was glad my son was out, and I had just had our family pictures taken for my parents. So I thought it was nice that they would have a picture of all of us together if I didn't make it out."

Denise tried talking to Fane while she was being held hostage. She thought that by making a connection with him she may increase her chances of survival.

"Was he receptive to talking to you?" I asked.

"I think at some points he was. But then at other times he was, you know, just out there like that mentally."

As the hours wore on, Denise said that Fane became easier to deal with on bathroom breaks. The remaining four hostages were females, so Fane probably realized, even in his altered state, that it was much easier to give in to the hostages' requests rather than deal with the aftermath.

Denise was one of the pawns used to pick up the food delivered to the front door by the ERU officers.

"He was behind me, and he had the gun on me. I just remember he would open the door, and I had to bend down and reach for the bag and grab it—and then we would back away from the door. He was using me as a shield as he was opening the door."

The food was delivered at different times and consisted of pizza, bread, bologna, and mayonnaise.

Reflecting now, I asked Denise if she knew there were ERU snipers watching her pick up the food, ready to shoot Michael Fane if the shot presented itself.

"I would have never volunteered to go to the door and do that. I never imagined there were snipers," she said.

BUILDING A TIME MACHINE

Fane allowed the hostages to converse during the ordeal. It consisted mostly of small talk and certainly nothing that could potentially set Fane into a fit of rage. He spent most of the time with the police negotiators, bartering for the equipment needed to build his time machine.

Besides his initial demands of twelve-inch bolts, sheets of plexiglass, and X-Acto knives, his demands increased in seriousness.

At 7:43 p.m., almost five hours after he took the hostages, Fane began asking for three gallons of liquid nitrogen, which is normally used by doctors to remove unwanted skin, warts, and precancerous cells.

Asphyxiation occurs quickly if liquid nitrogen is spilled in a confined space. And most concerning to the negotiator was the fact that explosions can occur if liquid nitrogen is not handled properly.

Fane continued making threats to harm the hostages if his irrational demands were not met.

Family members of the hostages began flooding the area of the police perimeter. The local news stations were providing continual reports, and word of the siege spread like wildfire throughout the South Omaha community. Family was initially allowed to rally at Darby's Tavern where the police command post was set up. But this proved to be impractical and a hindrance to the command officers and negotiators trying to talk to the suspect.

A Metro Area Transit city bus was called to the scene, and the family members were taken to a nearby church where they had warmth, food and drink, and clergy to help them with their stress. They also had access to a television with continually updated reports on what their loved ones were enduring inside the salon.

Still among the hostages, Darla wrote later about conditions inside the salon: "By now we had a TV in the room so as to keep track of news reports. One of the first reports upset me so when I saw our loved ones being loaded on a bus, and I caught a glimpse of our youngest son. So hard I can't describe.

"Another time stands out in my memory when the TV station talked of discontinuing power to the salon. That was very upsetting, but especially to Michael, and he got right on the phone and started yelling at the negotiator. He later calmed down a little and eventually told [the negotiator] to 'go ahead and shut off the power, it wouldn't make any difference.'"

NEGOTIATIONS REACH A DANGEROUS LEVEL

As the evening progressed, police officers with scopes were able to observe hostages lying on the floor of the salon with pillows. Michael Fane continued to talk to them, with the gun always in his hand.

Darkness had fallen, and the streetlights were not affording enough illumination on the salon. High-intensity portable lights were brought in. Soon the area resembled daylight.

Additional drop-offs of food were made to the front door by the ERU officers. Each time, the snipers studied Fane intently to see how the hostage picked up the bag and took it back into the salon, potentially exposing Fane for a kill shot.

During one of the food deliveries, it was apparent to the surveillance officers that Fane did not lock the front door after the bag was taken back into the salon. But would the ERU officers dare rush into the salon and try to rescue the hostages?

The decision was not to do a dynamic entry into the salon. It was too dangerous, given that Fane always had the gun in his hand and a bomb within feet of the hostages.

At 10:24 p.m. Fane must have realized his mistake. Officers watched him wrap a phone cord around the front door.

The negotiations became tense. Fane told the negotiator that he was a student of hostage negotiations. He emphasized he had no time frame for him to build his time machine, and he was in this situation for the duration. He made it clear he was not planning on releasing any of the remaining hostages.

He asked for a pickup truck and, again, liquid nitrogen.

Negotiations reached a dangerous level toward midnight.

SNIPERS GET A GREEN LIGHT

At 11:40 p.m. the ERU command officer told the snipers to take a shot on Fane if the situation presented itself. The snipers did not need the green light from their superiors if they felt that Fane could be neutralized without harm coming to the hostages.

By 1:56 a.m. the tone changed, and some progress was being made. There was talk between Fane and the negotiator about releasing a hostage. Fane was backing down from his demand of a pickup truck and liquid nitrogen being delivered prior to any hostage coming out.

At this point the important decision was made by command officers not to shoot Fane if the opportunity presented itself. Though kept in their positions, the snipers were instructed to stand down for the time being. Fane was making an important concession by agreeing to release a hostage.

At 2:20 a.m., after being held hostage for twelve hours, Denise was released by Michael Fane in exchange for a pack of cigarettes. There was now hope that perhaps Fane would wear down after close to twelve hours in the salon and release the remaining three hostages.

During my interview with Denise in 2016, she talked slowly and deliberately about her time in the salon.

"I did feel bad for the other hostages because they were having to stay there, you know? But I felt really good for me. I remember when they let me out the door, somebody grabbed me and handcuffed me [per police procedure] and took me over to this bar."

"What did you think about being handcuffed?"

"I thought it was strange," she said.

She described Fane's demeanor in the salon as quiet, irrational, and threatening. "I think he was just mentally not there."

During her time as a hostage Denise recalled one of the others asking Fane if they could write letters to their families.

He agreed, and Denise took the letters with her upon her release.

She also talked about the long-term ramifications this event has had on her life, even thirty years later.

Denise still cannot get the image out of her head when she was strapped to the suitcase that Fane repeatedly said carried a bomb. She said, "That's even scarier than having a gun on you,

you know, because if you're handcuffed to a bomb, there's no getting out."

A few years back Denise was at a Walgreens and saw a guy that dressed like and resembled Michael Fane. "I looked at him and I had to immediately leave and just get out the door because it just reminded me of the situation."

At the end of our interview I commended Denise for her courage and resolve during the hostage incident. After all, not everybody can say they were zip-tied to a suitcase containing a bomb.

She reminded me, "When you are in that situation, you have no choice."

Please make sure the people are praying not only for us, but for Michael. That God will touch him and the Holy Spirit will lift him out of whatever unpleasantness has caused him to do this.

Hostage letter written to family on Friday, December 30, 1988, from inside the hair salon.

I love you all. That's all I can really think about. Please pray for us to guide us through this ordeal. Kids: Mommy loves you and if I never see you again Daddy will be there. Your lives will be filled with so much love. Please never forget about me.

Hostage letter written to family on Friday, December 30, 1988, from inside the hair salon.

BIZARRE REQUESTS

The late night of December 29, 1988, soon crossed over into the darkness and coldness of the early morning. ERU officers and other perimeter officers were being relieved in shifts to experience the warmness of nearby Darby's Tavern, the command post used during the siege.

Michael Fane was still holding three female hostages after the release of Denise. His list of bizarre demands for the time machine materials was growing to include

- Numerous sheets of plexiglass
- Several 2 x 4 pieces of wood
- A roll of chicken wire
- Numerous nuts and bolts
- Various lengths of metal pipes
- End caps for the pipes
- Three gallons of liquid nitrogen

At 2:16 a.m. police officers were startled to hear what sounded like a gunshot from inside the hair salon. The police negotiator tried to reestablish contact with Michael Fane, with no initial success. Panic set in, and command officers running the operation began discussing potentially breaching the building to rescue the remaining three hostages.

Fortunately, at 2:32, Fane picked up the phone and stated everything was fine. It was verified the hostages were safe.

It was never determined what the noise that sounded like a gunshot was. But the hostages later said that Fane did not fire his weapon during the siege.

Negotiations with Fane were up and down throughout the night. Mood swings were common. Fane would threaten hostages during one conversation and then conduct a rational conversation minutes later with the negotiator.

The Omaha Police psychologist was monitoring the conversation with the police negotiator, and he was becoming concerned that Fane's mental state was changing and that the hostages may be at risk.

Throughout the ordeal more and more information was being learned about Michael Fane. His family claimed that Fane's IQ was 160, which is considered by many to be at the genius level. He apparently had recently lost a girlfriend over his use of illegal narcotics. Fane's family had tried treatment programs for their son, but counseling was unsuccessful.

Also, it was learned that Fane had recently been kicked out of his apartment that he shared with friends over his inability to pay rent. Of concern was Fane's fascination with bombs, which had recently grown into an obsession.

As a teenager, he was a fan of the book titled *The Anarchist Cookbook* written by William Powell and first published in 1971 at the height of the protests against the Vietnam War. The book provided "recipes" for Molotov cocktails and LSD, among other counterculture activities.

The Anarchist Cookbook has been linked to the Columbine school shooting and the Oklahoma City bombing, as well as other acts of violence.

Family members advised of a strained relationship between Fane and his father, mostly over the use of drugs.

The police psychologist later stated in a police report that "people felt this was significantly out of character for him in terms of becoming violent and imposing his will on other people. Although, the mother and father both told me that he [Michael Fane] is very manipulative, is basically lacking in conscience, and believed that society owed him a living."

Family members also said that in the week prior to the hostage siege, Michael Fane was talking about the book of Revelation in the Bible. The author of the book of Revelation, Saint John the Divine, offers a transcription of seven letters and later describes strange beasts, visions of judgments, governments, demonic battles, heaven, and a new world order—in other words, a prophetic vision for the end of the world.

Of concern was information from the family that Michael Fane was obsessed with bombs.

The police psychologist later stated how Fane was overheard by family members saying that "it would be fun to bomb something and to blow something up."

Why in the world was this not reported to law enforcement or to a mental health professional earlier? How many mass killings around this country had early warning signs ignored by those closest to the perpetrator?

The answer is too many.

A LUNATIC ON A MISSION

Throughout the twenty-four hours of negotiations, Fane made it clear that he was building a time machine with the materials he wanted police to supply him. The police psychologist was concerned with the alarming comments by Fane that he would incrementally release hostages but the last remaining hostage would be traveling with him on the time machine to a location he was refusing to supply.

As negotiations continued, the mental state of Fane became more apparent to the police psychologist who reported later, "I had the sense he was on a mission, had to accomplish this, and at the conclusion he was indifferent. His indifference over that led me to think that he either did not believe he was going to survive it, or he was going to take his own life or have us take his life. His own life meant relatively little to him."

The police negotiators and other command staff were convinced during conversations with Fane, and with additional information from his family, that he had constructed a functional explosive device in the red suitcase. The Omaha Police Department bomb squad was ready to act.

At 8:02 a.m. on Friday, Michael Fane released two more female hostages. The police negotiator bartered hostages for food, cigarettes, and other items that Fane had been requesting that, in the command officer's opinions, would pose no danger to hostages.

Now Fane held one last hostage inside the Possibilities Hair Salon. Law enforcement officials at the scene knew this would be the toughest one to negotiate release for because Fane had already indicated that the last hostage would be traveling with him on his time machine.

Darla wrote later how Fane chose which hostages would be released: "To choose who would leave, Fane placed three perm rods in a box and let the three of us draw. The person to get a different color would remain. I knew before I drew it would be me. When the two were released about 8:30 a.m. Friday was a very low point for me. But God was preparing me for the hardest thing I've ever been through."

THE LONE HOSTAGE

She told police, "The hardest time for me was when my friends left me. I didn't know when I'd get out of there."

Darla wrote later, "After the last two hostages left, I told God I could not handle this by myself, and I turned everything in my despair over to him. It was truly at that point when I felt a peacefulness settle over me. A comfort surrounded me, and I knew it was the Holy Spirit. I knew everything was in God's hands whether I lived or died."

All the other released hostages described Darla as being cool, calm, and collected during the ordeal. In fact, a police report quoted her as saying, "I really feared that there was something not too good in the suitcase. I wanted to ask him what it was, but I was afraid to. His motive was not robbery. I personally told him that the register had money in it, and he could have cared less."

Fane was forming an attachment to Darla and began telling her bits and pieces of his life that he had not yet revealed to the negotiator. He talked of his rocky relationship with his father.

"He'd never got along with his dad very good," she later told police, "but he told me he loved his dad."

Fane was a chain smoker and kept up the pace the entire time he was holding hostages.

Darla said, "He was determined to build whatever God instructed him to."

Fane used zip ties to secure her to a chair so he could sleep. However, it was quickly apparent to Fane that he was wide awake, and he then released her from the ties.

To keep her under his control, Fane forced her to go to the restroom with him. She wrote, "He took me inside with him and shut the door. (It had been seventeen hours since he had gone to the bathroom.) I turned toward the wall as he went."

She was also forced by Fane three times that day to go to the door and pick up supplies dropped off by the police. Each time Fane clutched her from behind, with his gun in her back.

Darla described the process like this: "We would approach the front door of the salon with the gun in my back and his hand at the neck of my shirt three times. I was always instructed to get down on my hands and knees, push open the door, and reach out to pull in the sack. I asked Fane to please not discharge the gun accidentally, because I feared the worst in his nervous state.

"At one point before we approached the door for the third time, I begged Michael to let me go for my family. I could see by the expression on his face he was sorry, but he told me he had no intention of letting me go because I was his only security."

"THIS GIRL ISN'T GOING TO GET TO LEAVE"

The police negotiator realized early in the afternoon of Friday that Fane was becoming more agitated and irritable. In a police report, he wrote, "Michael was very, very, adamant that the final hostage was not going to be released because that was his security. At approximately 1 or 2 o'clock the discussion with Michael became heated. At one point Michael began to threaten people more seriously and included the fact that he would harm the other hostage that was inside if we didn't meet his demands."

Fane was becoming more incoherent. He was not receiving the material he was requesting for his time machine.

The police log showed the following:

12:32 pm: Fane told the police negotiator that if the police try to enter the salon, he will press the trigger on his bomb and kill people.

1:03 pm: He says, "Tell the boss to stop fucking around. This girl isn't going to get to leave the building."

1:09 pm: Fane told the negotiator his mission is "more important than his life, her life, or your life."

1:16 pm: He threatened that he could be very ugly if he did not receive his "time machine" materials, and that he was on a mission from God.

1:22 pm: Fane allowed the lone hostage to talk to the police negotiator: *"I'm okay. I'm okay. Please give him what he wants and tell my family I'm okay."*

At 1:45 p.m. Fane told the negotiator that he had wired his bomb to the front door. The situation was deteriorating quickly. Fane still had one hostage and was armed with a handgun and a bomb.

Decisions needed to be made.

SEVER THE SPINAL CORD

Sniper Randy Eddy was being pressured by his command officers. They were demanding he give them a rock-solid assurance that his shot from 110 feet away would strike Michael Fane in the head.

Eddy was still somewhat defiant during my interview with him, in preparation for writing this story. He said, "They wanted me to give them 100 percent that this whole thing would go our way. No, I can't give you 100 percent. There are too many variables."

Eddy was worried about Fane consistently having his gun trained on the hostage's back or head. Eddy's plan was to deploy his bullet and sever Fane's spinal cord. This would cause instantaneous death and would reduce the chance that Fane's reflex motion would cause him to pull the trigger on his gun and shoot the hostage as a reaction.

"It's called flaccid paralysis," Eddy explained to me. "The spinal cord connects into the brain. If you are able to sever that [the T-Zone, the point where the spine connects to the brain], all motor functions cease instantly."

"And you're trained on this?" I asked.

"Yes."

Officer Eddy had also been trained on shooting high-powered rounds into glass. However, he made it clear to his superiors that he was worried about trying to shoot Fane through the front glass doors, since rounds can deflect in glass.

"From my experience shooting through glass, the bullet will not have a true trajectory."

The plan was simple. Fane was ordering more supplies. The package would be laid by the front door. Fane would use the last hostage as a shield to pick up the package. If Officer Eddy had a shot, he was now ordered to take it due to Fane's deteriorating mental condition and his escalation of threats toward the hostage.

Officer Eddy was positioned on the driveway of a house south of the front doors of the salon. He was partially hidden under a van parked in the driveway. Due to his black uniform it was unlikely that Fane could have spotted him looking out from the salon.

Eddy's rifle scope was precisely proficient in magnifying the suspect's head. He was focused on the distance between the suspect's face and the head of the hostage.

On the other side of the van was Omaha Police Officer Greg Stanzel, a ten-year veteran and fellow member of the elite Emergency Response Unit. Stanzel was the spotter for Eddy.

It was the spotter's job to "paint the picture" for Eddy by describing what was happening outside the narrow view of the rifle scope. Stanzel was an integral part of this operation.

Officer Eddy was ready and in position.

He described the scene for me: "So picture the [front] tire of this vehicle. It's sunny out when this went down. All that was exposed was my rifle barrel and just part of my face. If he [Fane] was to even look, that's the only thing he would see."

Officers Eddy and Stanzel had a deep conversation prior to getting into position.

Eddy said, "I told my spotter Greg Stanzel to watch the gun. I said, 'Greg, that's all I want you to do. We need to keep the radio clear. I want you to tell me when the gun is not pointed at her head.'"

Officer Eddy wanted no confusion before he pulled the trigger.

"I want you to say the words *on* or *off*. *On*, meaning it [the gun] is pointed at her head. *Off* means it's not pointed. Let's keep it simple."

The plan was set. Snipers were in place. Teams of ERU officers were ready to deliver the package of food to the front door.

Everybody was aware of the plan except two people: Michael Fane and his lone hostage.

Vantage point of sniper Randy Eddy toward the front door of Possibilities Hair Salon.

THAT SPLIT-SECOND LIFE-AND-DEATH DECISION

At 2:43 p.m.—nearly twenty-four hours after Michael Fane entered the hair salon—he led his hostage to the front doors of the salon for yet another package pickup.

Fane had done this before with Darla and other hostages. Food, cigarettes, and material to build his time machine had been previously delivered. During each of the handovers, the snipers had noticed different mannerisms of Fane while he held his gun to the back or head of the hostages. The snipers were looking for any weaknesses of Fane's that they could capitalize on.

The negotiation for this package had been difficult. Negotiators feared that Fane was planning to build another bomb instead of a time machine. The requests for liquid nitrogen and metal pipes with end caps were concerning. The fact that he was not going to receive these items caused frustrations that threatened his already erratic behavior.

Just earlier Fane had told police that after this delivery was made, he was going to sleep for a while and that he would not harm the hostage. During this conversation he was told, as a measure of good faith, not to point the gun at the hostage during the pickup of the package.

Now it was time.

The package was ready to be picked up outside the front door of the salon. Fane grabbed Darla by the neck of her blouse and held his gun in his other hand.

"He made it known to me that I shouldn't try anything funny," she said in a police report. "I was afraid the gun would go off accidentally, because he would be pretty nervous."

Fane led the lone hostage to the door and didn't like where the package was. He had the police reposition it to a spot where there was less danger for him to be taken out.

He again led the hostage to the door, had her open it, and they stepped out a few steps.

"He had control over me," Darla recalled.

Randy Eddy, the sniper, was focused during my interview with him in 2016. I could only imagine how fixated he was lying in that driveway in 1988.

He told me, "So everybody's in place. We're all set up. He [an officer] drops the sack right there a couple of feet from the door. All the rest [of the deliveries] have been right up against the door."

I asked, "What's Fane doing when the food is being delivered?"

"When the food is being delivered, I don't see him, and I don't see the hostage either. I don't know where they are at. Every time they did this, I didn't see them until the lunch team [the ERU officers delivering the food and supplies] had left," he explained.

"Well, he comes up and he's got the gun to her head, he's got her by the back of the collar and he looks and he backs out of the entryway and then a few minutes, or probably a few seconds later, the negotiator gets on the radio, and said, 'There's something he doesn't like, the sandwich is too far away. What are you guys doing?'

"Shit, dammit.

"So the ERU commander got on the radio and said move it closer. The guys moved back up [and moved the package closer to the doorway]."

"But you lost your two- or three-second advantage?" I asked.

"We did. They go up and they move it right up against the door and then they flanked back out. So now the sandwich is set up, he comes out. Then they come to the door, the sandwiches are on the ground right there, she's [leaning over] and he's hunkered down behind her and he's got the gun to her head.

"So they come to the door, she opens the door, he's got the gun to her head, and I'm listening to Greg, *on, on, on*, so she reaches out, grabs it, pulls it, and the door shuts. At that point, he's inside the door and she kind of arcs up a little bit and then he kind of stands up and when he stops, his face is right behind this metal thing [push bar] and I remember thinking shit. I remember thinking that, but then for some reason, he stood up a little bit more, and I heard Greg say *off*.

"Boom. The shot went right above that bar, and I saw him go down.

"As soon as the shot went off, they [other officers] reached in and they grabbed her, and I remember seeing her head covered in blood.

"I remember for two seconds, I thought I hit her. I thought, because her head was right below his chin when he arced up and she was kind of right in front of him. I saw the blood. I thought she was hit, and then I saw the guys grab her and I saw her get up on her own power.

"Mark, I can't tell you that feeling of relief, of okay, maybe she's injured, but she's not dead, she's alive. I even asked Greg, 'Stanzel, do you think she was hit?'"

At this point in the interview, I had a million questions. I asked Eddy, "But they are inside when you fired the shot?"

He said, "Yeah, the door is closed, and they were inside."

"And she's up against his body or close to his body?"

"I remember seeing her below the chin, and I remember that bar, she was below it, and he was right above it. I could see her head right below it."

"Where did you place the shot then?" I asked.

"Right at the edge of the left eye. The bullet had, like we knew, broke up on entry. The largest chunk of the bullet hit him right next to the bridge of the nose, into the brain, and I don't know if we achieved flaccid paralysis. The bullet went where I wanted it to, but I don't know. They said he was dead instantly. He fell backward," Eddy said.

"The placement of the shot would have been about six inches above her head?"

"I'd say that's a pretty good guess."

"Tell me what you did after the shot."

Eddy said, "I didn't know if she was hit with a bullet fragment. All I know was she was alive, she was up and running on her own power, she was alive and after that I didn't care, whether she lost an eye, she was cut, you know what, you're alive, we got you out of there alive. And he was not moving, because I was really afraid if he was able to crawl a couple of feet and hit whatever activator switch and detonate the bomb.

"But he wasn't moving. They jumped in, they handcuffed him right away, and we had made the decision, prior to the incident, the four of us, the two snipers and the two spotters, no matter what happens here, no matter what happens, when this is done, the four of us are going to meet up and we are walking back to the command post, together, all four of us, and that's what we did."

"And you didn't walk over and see the body?"

"Never did."

Eddy also noted, "I didn't realize until six months later that when I finally fired that shot, my bullet went about eight inches by a police officer's head because he was right up against the wall there."

Omaha Police investigator standing over the body of Michael Fane, in the entryway of the Possibilities Hair Salon. (Reprinted with permission of the Omaha World-Herald.*)*

DARLA'S ANGELS

Inside the salon, Darla had watched as the officers moved the package closer to the front door on Fane's insistence.

She wrote later, "We approached the door. I got down on my hands and knees and pushed open the door, but this time was different, I had to reach further, the sack was much heavier, and I had to almost lie on my right side.

"I had the sack and started to pull it to me and then there was a loud pop.

"The glass shattered in front of me, and as I turned slightly to my left to look, I saw Michael Fane fall back. I momentarily thought: Is he gonna shoot? I then heard my name, and two angels of mercy pulled me out of my temporary hell into the air and ran with me, one on each side, talking, talking, telling me I was okay and I was out of there."

The final hostage, being whisked to safety by members of the elite Emergency Response Unit of the Omaha Police Department. (Reprinted with permission of the Omaha World-Herald.)

WE ALL THOUGHT IT WAS A REAL FIREARM

Knowing how important support of family is during tough times on duty, I asked Eddy this: "I don't want to get involved in any personal things you don't want to, but I'm going to ask you the question. Tell me what Kim [Eddy's wife] was like when you got home."

"I walked in," he said. "We lived in a split-level house. I walked to the top of the stairs, and I just remember hugging my wife for a long time. Relief that all of our guys got out of it without getting hurt, all the hostages were released and none of them were hurt, tragic that there was a loss of life, you know, this young man, but he brought it on himself. You know, as a police officer, people think that police officers wake up every day thinking they want to go out and shoot somebody, which is absolutely not the case. It's the absolute last resort to take a human life, but if that's what you have to do to save another life, then that's what we have to do."

Kim Eddy remembers that day: "Just then, the cruiser with Randy pulled up. I could feel the tears welling up in my eyes. Randy reached out for me and gave me the biggest hug ever. We stood there for what seemed to be hours. The fear of reliving this experience will always be with me, but the fear of something worse happening is on my mind too. I can't help but wonder what would have happened if Randy had not killed Michael Fane."

I asked Eddy about the pressure on him: "You had more pressure on you than most officers have, that I know of, in their officer-involved shootings because you had an innocent life within six inches of where you had to fire the shot."

He said, "I don't think I had more pressure, but I had more time to think about it before it happened. Most officer-involved shootings are instantaneous, it's on the fly, we are going right now, we are reacting. I had time to think about it."

"And it turned out to be a pellet gun that looked exactly like a real firearm," I said.

"I thought it was a real gun. We all thought it was a real firearm. I wish I could have seen it better. It would have changed a lot of things," Eddy said.

Any Omaha Police officer involved in a line-of-duty death is required to appear before a grand jury to determine if the officer should be charged with any crime for the actions they took. I asked him about how the grand jury inquiry went.

"Good," he said. "The dumbest question I was asked was why didn't you shoot the gun out of his hand? That's just Hollywood."

Three decades after Randy Eddy killed Michael Fane, he ended the interview with this observation: "I think for the first year, it was the first thing I thought about in the morning and last thing I thought about before I went to sleep. Did it bother me that I killed the guy? Yes and no. I wish we could have got all the hostages out, put this guy in a mental institution, but the situation as it was, we did our job. It was the only way to resolve this. I don't regret what I did.

"Am I proud of killing him? No.

"Am I proud that I could put my round where it needed to be? Yeah, I am proud of that."

FROM THE SPOTTER'S POINT OF VIEW

Officer Greg Stanzel, the spotter, had been positioned on the other side of the van from where Randy Eddy took the fatal shot.

He gave the final *off* call over the radio, signaling to Eddy that now was the time to take the shot.

"I had a pair of binoculars and a spotting scope," Stanzel recalled during my interview with him. "My job was to be the main communicator of information once the suspect entered the vestibule. The negotiations had deteriorated to the point where they [the negotiators] didn't think this hostage was going to come out unharmed."

Stanzel positioned himself about six feet away from Eddy, and they communicated by radio. His vantage point allowed him a reliable picture of everything that would occur in the vestibule, once the suspect came out with the hostage.

Stanzel recalls watching Michael Fane when he and the hostage appeared in the doorway.

He said, "They immediately went to their knees, just like the previous package deliveries. He [Fane] had the gun in his right hand. It appeared to be a high-capacity semi-automatic pistol, like a Beretta 92. The gun was pointed into the back of the hostage's neck in such a way that she was grimacing a bit. You could tell it hurt.

"The hostage pushes the front door open. His head is exposed above her head, but the gun is still pointed at her neck. She has to get her elbow all the way out the door to reach the [package] so she starts to separate herself from the suspect. He kept the gun attached to the back of her neck.

"And then, as she grabbed the item, he started to pull her back in. He started to rise up and the gun came away from her neck.

"The gun was just a little bit away from her, about 45 degrees from her neck. I didn't make the call for the shot right then because I didn't know exactly how long it was going to be before he got that gun back on her.

"But I realized that as he used his weight and momentum to stand up, he was getting farther away from the gun. At that time, I made the decision in my head that it's safe."

Officer Stanzel told Eddy to take the shot.

"I heard the shot and the top half of the exterior glass blew out. I could see the suspect get hit pretty much right in the face. He dropped immediately, just like a sack of potatoes. I knew immediately she had not been shot. She had a real shocked look on her face."

Stanzel was concerned about the welfare of his partner.

"I kind of slid up to Randy and said, 'Good job, are you all right?' He was okay, and we laid there for a second, just kind of thinking of what had happened here."

Greg Stanzel is a second cousin of mine. I asked him about the stresses and guilt he still feels from the verbal call he made that night, resulting in the death of Michael Fane: "Did you ever, when you were behind that van, think, shit, I don't want to make this call?"

He said, "You know, at the time, I didn't. But I'll be honest with you, since then I struggle with it a little bit. We didn't know all the stuff we know about him now. This kid was crazy. But I still know I did right. Because during the time, this kid looked like Charles Manson to me. The picture in the paper was a clean-cut picture from high school. But he was a ratty looking guy.

"It all boils down to … it needed to be done."

As Stanzel was telling this story, I came to realize the enormity of responsibility on his shoulders that day. His role was every bit as vital and important as that of the sniper, Randy Eddy.

"What you did is one of the ultimate decisions that a police officer has to make," I noted.

"Yeah, and it wasn't made in a split second. That's the difference between most of them [officer-involved shootings]. We went out knowing that if the opportunity presented itself, this is how it had to end. I mean, it was very businesslike when we did it."

He reiterated, "[Fane] put himself into a position that we didn't kill him. He killed himself."

I was struck by the heaviness that still permeates my second cousin's soul. His voice began cracking.

"I actually went to my priest, ten years later, and I said to him, 'I know I did the right thing, but if I didn't, I want forgiveness.'"

I am proud to have worked for many years with the likes of Omaha Police Officers Randy Eddy and Greg Stanzel. They trained for situations like the Fane hostage-taking scenario, and both were able to flawlessly carry out that mission. A hostage is still alive based on their actions.

THE AFTERMATH

The bomb squad inspected the red suitcase after Fane had been killed. The device in the suitcase consisted of a can of paint remover, a 6-volt battery, and several lead relay and toggle switches. The top of the paint remover can had been drilled into. Through this opening two wires were run into the well of the can and were taped to a flashbulb, which was immersed in the liquid inside of the can.

The officers determined that Fane had brought an incendiary device into the Possibilities Hair Salon capable of causing destruction, injuries, and death if he had detonated the device at any time during the hostage situation.

It seems like Fane had done his homework after learning to make the bomb from *The Anarchist Cookbook*. By the way, *The Anarchist Cookbook* can still be purchased on Amazon for those who want to construct a bomb.

The gun used by Fane was later determined to be a pellet gun, constructed to be a replica of a semi-automatic handgun.

Michael Fane's actions in December 1988 impacted more lives than his own. The hostages still bear scars. Just imagine being thrown into this surreal situation. How would you react to being zip-tied to a bomb? Or being six inches from a sniper's bullet, fired into the face of the man holding a gun to your back?

Darla wrote, "It's changed my life forever. I believe I witnessed a miracle, and I was held alone in that building. My life will never be the same."

A twenty-four-hour standoff, complete with incremental releases of hostages, threats of detonating a bomb, and demanding materials to build a time machine are more common for a Hollywood screenplay than an actual incident. This was no *Dog Day Afternoon*, and Al Pacino wasn't in town shooting a movie.

Yet Officers Eddy and Stanzel answered the call. They did the right thing.

Some may wonder why I chose to write about this story. After all, I wasn't there during the entire incident. In fact, earlier that day I requested the use of the Emergency Response Unit to help me and my crew serve a high-risk search warrant for a crack cocaine operation. (Obviously, the incident at the hair salon trumped my crack cocaine warrant.)

I wrote this story because I can identify with split-second decisions on taking a person's life.

Whether a single shot is fired to end a hostage situation or, like in my case, thirty-two shots are fired in thirteen seconds from mere feet away toward a drug dealer we were chasing and who fired on us, police officers are forced every day to make life-altering decisions.

Cops are human. Some make the wrong decision and lives are lost. But Eddy and Stanzel made the right decision, under difficult circumstances, resulting in a life being saved. They are still heroes, thirty-two years later.

3

TITS AND ASS

In 1980 I was a young uniformed Omaha Police officer assigned to District 155 in the west central portion of the city. It was around 11:30 on a busy Friday night, and I was soon due to be called in by the dispatcher to officially complete my shift.

It was summertime and I'm sure I was looking forward to peeling off my sweaty bulletproof vest and heading to the Treehouse Lounge for a cold one with my buddies.

I received a call of traffic congestion near 72nd and Hartman Avenue. The dispatcher reported cars were at a standstill, which most likely meant a stalled vehicle or a car accident.

The north-south 72nd Street was a major four-lane thoroughfare, with the ever-expanding Immanuel Medical Center just a short distance to the north of Hartman Avenue. To the west of 72nd Street was a huge open field known as the tower farm—a prominent high hill where multiple antenna-type towers reaching over 1,300 feet in height were situated and that broadcast the local television stations in Omaha.

On the east side of 72nd was the Sky View Drive-In theater. Opened in 1954, the Sky View was a popular place for families and teens to take in some of the most popular movies of the time.

The screen was eighty feet tall, and the drive-in could host over a thousand vehicles. To the east of the outdoor theater was a neighborhood of houses. The intersection of 69th Avenue and Ogden was a dead end and looked out over the large landscape of the Sky View.

After dark, neighbor kids frequently took over this dead end to watch the movies for free. If the wind was blowing in the right direction, they could even hear the words. I have also heard stories how the more technologically advanced teen could rig their own speaker to pick up the waves from the drive-in broadcast.

I recall my big sister, Judi, and her husband, Mike, taking me to the Sky View in 1970 to see Jack Lemmon and Sandy Dennis in *The Out-of-Towners*, a great comedy that I still watch when I channel surf onto it today.

The Sky View provided good, wholesome family time with the chance to enjoy a cool breeze and popcorn after a stifling hot and humid summer day in Omaha.

Cars traveling north and south on 72nd Street had full view of the movie being shown. Occasionally, I would shag a car off the median or curb who wanted to watch a movie for free.

Soon after receiving my radio call, I arrived in the area. As soon as I turned onto 72nd, I could not believe my eyes. There were cars stopped in both directions. All four lanes of traffic were blocked, and cars were parked on the middle median and over the outside curbs.

People were standing outside their cars, all peering in the same direction toward the busy Sky View screen. I was barely able to navigate my police cruiser through the throngs as I attempted to determine what was causing the gridlock.

Never had I ever seen a backup of traffic like this at the Sky View.

I turned my head toward the same direction as the others and saw an eighty-foot video of a couple engaged in extremely amorous activity. I had never seen a movie like this being shown at the Sky View. The female actress's boobs were in full display, as well as her ass feigning an up-and-down motion on the male actor's naked body. Though actual genitalia were not shown, believe me when I say that this movie left little to the imagination.

The sexual movie caused a total traffic jam so gridlocked that nobody was moving. Also, I found it fascinating that nobody appeared to want to move.

I was powerless to do anything but sit in my cruiser and enjoy the flick with the other hundred or so cars parked along 72nd Street.

Soon the movie was over, and the cars moved on. I went to the office to advise the manager of the traffic jam that occurred based on the "nudie" movie being shown in full display of the neighborhood. I recall how apologetic he was. It seems that he failed to view the movie prior to showing it, and he had no idea of the realistic sex scenes it portrayed. He promised to be more vigilant in the future.

Keep in mind this was close to forty years ago, well before the introduction of internet porn. Movies like this were not nearly as easy to come by. The people in those cars going up and down 72nd Street had to be shocked when they saw the love-making in full display.

Fortunately, I didn't respond to any "rear-end" collisions that evening.

4

THE REAL HELLS ANGELS— THE STREET VERSION OF THE *SONS OF ANARCHY*

The low, deep-throated rumble of Harley-Davidsons with their riders—members of the Hells Angels Motorcycle Club—cruising two by two, roaring down the street, would often cause traffic to pull over and citizens to gawk. A Hells Angels motorcycle procession was akin to a presidential motorcade.

For us, as Omaha cops, the thundering processions were less distracting than their criminal behavior because we knew the club members were active in selling methamphetamine while ruling the streets through intimidation and fear.

The aura of the Hells Angels was undeniable. Large bearded men riding Harley-Davidson motorcycles while wearing leather vests with the Hells Angels patches sewn on the back created an atmosphere of invincibility among the members and followers.

To many criminals, the Hells Angels achieved a rock star status akin to being the gangster John Gotti of motorcycle gangs.

As a rookie cop in the late 1970s, I frequently saw Hells Angels riding up and down 30th Street in North Omaha—a rougher part of town, north of downtown. There were several bars in the neighborhood known to cater to the Angels. On Friday nights I would see dozens of tricked-out Harleys lined up perfectly in front of the establishments, almost daring anybody to touch them.

I learned that Hells Angels should not be taken lightly when they were riding in a pack. Most likely there were guns and drugs somewhere in that motorcycle procession. However, the Angels were extremely street savvy not to get caught. They tried to follow all the traffic laws, and even if they didn't, what lone cop was going to stop a dozen dangerous guys on Harleys by himself?

The Hells Angels may have been criminals, but they were no dummies.

I also deduced that the strength of the Hells Angels was in their numbers, but when alone, they were vulnerable. I am sure most Hells Angels from that era would probably have said the same about Omaha Police officers.

In 1979, on a humid summer evening my partner and I responded to a call at 30th and Curtis Avenue to assist an officer who had requested backup for a traffic stop. We were close and arrived minutes later. We saw a lone Hells Angels member sitting on his bike in front of the officer's cruiser. The Angel was known to be dangerous and a hothead.

We approached him while the original officer was writing a traffic ticket in his cruiser.

He was one of the smaller Hells Angels in stature, and skinny as a rail. His coal black hair was tied back in a ponytail, with his scraggily beard needing tending to.

Back in 1979 there was no required helmet law for motorcyclists, so the Angel simply wore a bandana and reflective sunglasses to complement his tight jeans and black T-shirt.

The back of his black leather vest displayed a half-circular patch with red lettering on a white background that stated *Hells Angels*. Below that in the middle was the famous death's head insignia of a helmeted white skull attached to yellow wings.

On the bottom of the back of his vest, directly below the death's head insignia, was a rectangular white patch with red letters spelling *Nebraska*.

The vest he wore left no doubt he was an active member of the Nebraska chapter of the Hells Angels outlaws—the real ones, not TV's *Sons of Anarchy*.

He was quite upset, and every other word out of his mouth was *fuck*.

"This is fucking bullshit!"

"I'll have your fucking badges."

"You fuckers like harassing me because I'm a fucking Hells Angel!"

It just didn't stop, and his conduct was bordering on really pissing my partner and me off.

Even though I was a rookie, I was learning the tough streets of North Omaha well. I realized the best way to defuse a volatile situation was through communication—the type of communication that people in tough neighborhoods understood.

So I looked at this Hells Angel and in a monotone said, "One more *fuck* out of your fucking mouth and you'll be going to fucking jail while riding in the back of that fucking police car. And then I'll call a fucking tow truck to tow that motherfucking motorcycle of yours, so shut the fuck up."

An uncomfortable silence.

Not another *fuck* came out of his mouth, and after he signed his ticket, he roared off into the sunset.

Current day police officers are at a disadvantage in handling similar situations. Everything they do is being recorded by body cameras or cruiser cameras or on citizens' cell phones.

I maintain my conduct was totally professional with the Angel. I was able to keep him from going to jail. This saved us the time of making all kinds of reports. Not arresting him also kept us on the streets to possibly save someone trapped in a burning car or to arrest an intoxicated husband who was about to be gutted by an equally infuriated wife who just caught him feeling up the fourteen-year-old stepdaughter.

It certainly made his life easier by not having to pay money to bond out of jail or for the tow charge on his beloved hog.

It was a win-win for all involved.

But imagine if that conversation had been recorded and played on CNN for all to hear. I would have had hell to pay. No police officer today with a bodycam would dare talk to a criminal like that. That's a huge tactical disadvantage in the difficult job of maintaining the peace.

TATTOOS AND A SECRET SAFE

During my career I was involved in two major investigations targeting the Omaha chapter of the Hells Angels.

In 1981 I was assigned to a court security detail for a federal trial of numerous Omaha Hells Angels, along with the wife of a deceased member, on the charges of drug distribution and weapons violations. For several weeks I assisted the US Marshals in transporting the prisoners to and from the courthouse. I also sat in the courtroom to assist with security.

Hells Angels from all over the country rode and flew in as a show of support. One wore a three-piece suit along with the Hells Angels vest showing he was an active member. It turns out he was the Hells Angels accountant. His job was to make sure the attorneys in Omaha were paid on time, most likely in cash.

One of the least favorite jobs each day was strip-searching the Angels who were on trial before they were allowed into the courtroom. Early on we were surprised to discover a spider tattoo on the penis of one of the Angels. He was one of the few who would talk to us, so I asked what prompted him to decorate his manhood in such an elaborate manner.

He said, "I was so fucked up, I don't even remember having it done."

The 1981 trial was a disappointment for law enforcement. The jury acquitted the defendants on many of the more serious charges, and the resulting prison sentences did little to impact the Omaha chapter's drug-dealing activities.

In 1990 a more substantial investigation was conducted involving the Douglas County Sheriff's Department (Omaha is in Douglas County in Nebraska), the FBI, and the Omaha Police Department. This resulted in the seizure of hundreds of thousands of dollars in money and drugs, along with numerous firearms.

Law enforcement officers, acting on a court order, covertly placed listening devices throughout the Waterloo, Nebraska, house of Hells Angels member Gary Apker. Waterloo is a small, rural western suburb of Omaha.

The bugs in Apker's house provided us much-needed information on those involved in the methamphetamine distribution operation. After all, where is the one location most criminals feel safe talking about selling drugs? In the bust we found Apker's secret safe containing over $200,000 in cash, weapons, and ten pounds of methamphetamine.

Numerous men and women, including Apker, were indicted and convicted. In 2016 Gary Apker was released from federal prison at the age of seventy-seven, after serving over twenty years.

The Hells Angels in Omaha were never the same.

THE HELLS ANGELS CODE

In 2016 I was able to establish contact with an individual who was a close associate of the Omaha Hell Angels in the 1980s and 1990s. I am not going into detail as to how this contact was made, who initiated it, or where our interview was conducted.

Rest assured, I knew of this guy for years as being a runner for the Omaha Hells Angels. He sold drugs for them, collected monies owed for drug sales, and was considered an enforcer for those who did not pay their debts. Although he was never made a full-fledged member of the club, he was still known to law enforcement as someone who needed to be watched.

Normally, when I write stories like this, I try to be as descriptive as possible. It is my obligation to the reader to paint a picture as to what this guy looks like, how he talks, his likes and dislikes, where and how he grew up, as well as his personal idiosyncrasies.

I cannot do that here, as it is paramount I keep his identity secret for his own personal safety. Hells Angels did not tolerate snitches, and I owe it to "Larry" to keep him safe.

Larry began the interview by setting the most important ground rules of the motorcycle club.

"The Hells Angels are not going to talk to you if you are not riding a Harley-Davidson and if you're not white," he told me. Larry was both of those, which gave him an immediate advantage.

"My first contact with the HA's motorcycle club was in 1979. The first time I tried crank [slang for methamphetamine] was at a bar with a Hells Angel who turned me on to some."

Larry was a tough dude who could hold his own in bar fights. Hells Angels were also known to raise some hell themselves in bars, so they appreciated a guy like him, who could kick the shit out of a guy during a bar brawl. That's how Larry got their attention.

"I had to straighten out a few messes from time to time, and the Angels were pretty comfortable with what they saw from me, I guess," he told me.

Larry was equally impressed with how Hells Angels gang members conducted themselves in bars. However, he quickly learned the code of conduct for dealing with members of the club.

"I learned you don't ever try to tell a Hells Angel what to do if you're not a Hells Angel. And if you've fucked with one of them, you've fucked with all of them. It was hard to tell what set them off," he said.

He described the treatment given to a guy who dared to challenge a Hells Angel member at the old Joker Lounge in Council Bluffs, Iowa, just across the river from Omaha.

"There were about four HA's and they just started to put the boots to him. They weren't stopping, and I finally stepped over the guy and said, 'Hey, this guy has had enough,' so they pulled me in and gave me some too."

The Hells Angels were forgiving to Larry, and soon he was riding with them from bar to bar. He felt like he was king of the world. He said, "It was like you were invincible, like you were bulletproof. People would get out of the way. Walking into a bar was like Moses parting the Red Sea."

Being only an associate had its disadvantages. "Of course, we were always in the back of the pack [of the Harley-Davidsons] because we were just friends and associates. But, man, it was one of the most impressive things to be a part of."

Larry surprisingly told me how the Angels enjoyed taking over bars not normally known for biker activity. One such tavern was in a trendy, upscale West Omaha neighborhood and was known more as being a meat market than for attracting outlaw motorcycle gangs.

"That was half the delight, going into bars like these and scaring the patrons," he said. Larry learned quickly who was in charge when the Hells Angels were around. "They do not appreciate anybody stealing their thunder. They like being the center of attention."

I was surprised when I asked Larry if members of the Hells Angels ever held quantities of methamphetamine themselves when they were out in public. He said, "Yeah, they did. And not just little quantities."

Larry said they felt invincible, and the possibility of a snitch in the group was remote at best. "Oh, there was no such thing as snitching. You would only do that once and not walk away from it."

He said it was fascinating to see the two distinct social worlds that Hells Angels members lived in. Most had wives and kids at home, and plenty of girlfriends and opportunities on the side. The secret to their sexual success was one thing—methamphetamine.

"It was rare for an Angel to bring a wife around to a party. There were two separate worlds, the girlfriends and the wives," he said. "Strippers were a good source of fun for the guys. They had low self-esteem issues anyway, and then they get around these guys—it's because they're Hells Angels. It's not because the guys were good-looking, and it's certainly not because they were nice guys. The girls felt like they were somebody, and the guys were constantly feeding drugs to them."

Larry viewed the strippers as property of the Hells Angels, and it was not a good idea for any nonmember to show attention to the girls. "You didn't want to chat one up, you know. You better be careful if she starts chatting you up."

I prodded Larry on how guys like him hooked up with the girls at Hells Angels parties.

"They'd say, hey, you go make out with that one there. They'd tell guys like me to stuff her nose full of dope and then she'd put on a hell of a show."

STRANGE DOINGS INSIDE THE CLUBHOUSE

I was curious about the parties the Angels frequently held at their clubhouse, which in the 1980s was in a poor neighborhood on Military Avenue on the north side of Omaha. It was an old two-story stucco house that set high from the main street. Parking was in the back and was reached through an alley. The club made no efforts to hide the location of their clubhouse. For years, a Hells Angels sign hung on the front of the house and was plainly visible from Military Avenue.

The Omaha Police Department conducted surveillance on parties over the years at the clubhouse. Many times, hundreds of Hells Angels from around the country would arrive for the weekend to commemorate significant anniversaries. The parties lasted all weekend and never seemed to stop.

Larry said, "We called the clubhouse Lake Street [since it was just south of the street by the same name]. It was ground zero for fine parenting. The ladies would drag their small children along and put these little kids in the upstairs bedrooms. Mom would be downstairs whoring for dope. It was pretty pathetic."

Larry has a sentimental side, especially when it comes to little kids. He said, "I was never relaxed at the clubhouse. I was always on edge, and it was never my favorite place to go."

He referred to the clubhouse as a zoo, with many fights occurring after the drug and alcohol use escalated. There were few rules when it came to parties at the clubhouse, but one in particular held no exceptions: "You could do all the dope you wanted, but you just couldn't use a needle."

During my many years as a drug cop for the Omaha Police Department, I knew that the worst type of methamphetamine user was the "banger"—slang for a druggie using a hypodermic needle. The effects are more drastic, and diseases like hepatitis and HIV/AIDS are more easily transmitted from person to person by using needles.

"With the Angels," he said, "you could do all the dope you wanted, you just couldn't use a needle. If you start banging, you can't trust a junkie. That's gospel for those guys."

Women were nothing less than sexual toys for the Hells Angels during the clubhouse parties, with wannabes like Larry picking up sloppy seconds.

"One of the strangest things I ever encountered at the clubhouse was when there was a hell of a party going on. I went upstairs to go to the bathroom. I shut the door and I'm just about ready to piss when the shower door comes open. There's this girl sitting in the tub buck naked and she says, 'Piss on me.' So I said, 'What?' and she goes, 'Pee on me.'"

He said, "She's soaking wet in piss, and I was like oh my God!"

It turns out the guys decided to engage in some golden shower action with a drugged-out stripper who was too high to even get out of the bathtub.

"Her hair was soaking wet, and she looked like she had just turned the shower on. I got the fuck out of there!"

Girls routinely served drinks in the nude, but since they were strippers anyway, it was not something too out of the ordinary. "Everybody was so wired that nobody could get a hard-on anyway. The doors were locked and there were plates of dope out."

Larry began buying methamphetamine on a regular basis from the Hells Angels, and this practice was not without its pitfalls. He told me the Hells Angels he dealt with regularly added inositol to the methamphetamine in order to reduce its purity. Inositol is a powdery agent that has many primary medical purposes such as dealing with nerve pain, insomnia, and attention deficit disorder.

I am certainly familiar with the use of such cutting agents as inositol by drug dealers. By adding the inositol, a white powder, to the methamphetamine, the dealer reduces the purity (which customers frown on) while at the same increasing the bulk amount of product to be sold (which allows dealers to realize a higher profit margin).

Larry said, "If I was buying in quantity, I could get a better deal from them. But there was better dope on the street."

He knew he had to be careful complaining to the Angels about the quality of their methamphetamine. He said, "I witnessed more than one guy get cuffed around for making the mistake of saying he could get better shit than this."

And Larry had another disadvantage when getting drugs from the Angels. "I personally was not the best dope dealer because I could party it up a lot of times faster than I could sell it." In other words, he liked to use the product more than he enjoyed selling it. "And these are not the guys you could go to and say, 'Look, I don't have your money.' I was smart enough to know that."

So Larry was careful when it came to buying methamphetamine from the Hells Angels. "The favorite weapon for the Hells Angels was the ball-peen hammer, because it fits in the sleeve of a jacket so nicely," and Larry never wanted to be on the receiving end.

Today the Hells Angels have a clubhouse in South Omaha.
This photo was taken in 2017.

Toward the end of our interview, I asked him to reflect on his time with the Hells Angels and any regrets he might have. His answer surprised me.

"I still respect the colors because they did have my back for a while. I didn't owe them anything, and they didn't owe me anything, but God damn, they were fun to be around," he said. "Oh my God, there were many people enamored with the Hells Angels."

There is currently an active chapter of the Omaha Hells Angels, though Larry has not associated with the club for over twenty-five years.

My final question to him was this: "Is it fair to say the Hells Angels were never the same after the 1991 investigation when we put listening devices in the Hells Angels house?"

"They all went away after that," Larry said. "There wasn't anybody left, and I just kind of went my own way and started going through other contacts for my dealing. You guys hurt them real good."

5

THE KINDERGARTEN CLASS'S MOST SURPRISING SHOW-AND- (LET'S NOT) TELL

I do not remember much of my kindergarten years at Minne Lusa Elementary School in North Omaha.

I recall my mom walking me down the enormous hill from 31st and Ida to the crosswalk located at the busy 30th Street, also known as Nebraska State Highway 75. To a five-year-old, 30th Street seemed like the Indianapolis 500 with cars constantly racing by in both directions. Drivers appeared frustrated when the light turned red for a scrawny kindergartner to cross the street holding his metal lunch box, ready to walk two blocks on his own to the massive red-brick building that housed Mrs. Brown's morning kindergarten class.

Can you imagine allowing your five-year-old to walk two blocks alone to school today?

By far my favorite day was show-and-tell. Every kindergartner relishes the idea of bringing the coolest and most unique item to show off to the other kids. Whether it's a toy truck for the boys, a new Barbie for the girls, or even a rare coin from the 1800s, showing and telling was both fun and important in that it forced shy little kids to verbalize why they brought what they did.

There was an added factor for my show-and-tell days. By the time I was in kindergarten my brother, Tom, and sister, Judi, were grown adults and out of the house. Over the years they have loved to rib me about how spoiled I allegedly was, being that I was a late-in-life baby. From my young perspective I was an only child while growing up.

So, as hard as it is to admit to Tom and Judi, I did have some cool stuff to take to show-and-tell days, such as a toy tow truck and a miniature police car with lights and sirens. Best of all was my Batman outfit complete with a mask, cape, and utility belt with a batarang—a bat-shaped throwing weapon used to knock guns out of an assailant's hand.

In the late 1980s, while I was a detective in the narcotics unit, I received one of my strangest and most bizarre assignments, which harkened me back to my show-and-tell days at Minne Lusa School.

I was sent by my sergeant to a West Omaha elementary school. For those readers not from Omaha, West Omaha is far removed from the poverty-stricken neighborhoods that line block after block in the North Omaha area.

This school was surrounded by lovely two-story homes with beautifully landscaped yards and lush thick trees that offered shady spots all summer long.

In contrast, many North Omaha schools sat in high-crime areas encircled by vacant lots, broken liquor bottles, wrecked cars, and a sense of hopelessness that a better life, though only a few miles away in West Omaha, seemed to be as far away as the moon.

In 1971, the US Supreme Court ruled that federal courts could order busing to integrate public schools. In 1976, a federal court order mandated busing in the Omaha Public School

System, allowing African American kids from North Omaha to experience a better life, albeit for a few hours each day.

So when I was sent to that West Omaha school to investigate a claim from a teacher of suspicious activity involving one of her kindergartners, my curiosity was raised.

It turns out it was show-and-tell day in the class, and the kids were all excited about what they brought to share. The class was a mixture with kids from both the West Omaha neighborhood near the school and those bused in every day from North Omaha. One of the North Omaha kids sat anxiously while waiting to be called on by the teacher.

I'm sure the other kids had new toys to show off, or maybe a stamp collection or baseball cards of George Brett or Ozzie Smith. When it finally came to the five-year-old boy from North Omaha, he pulled out a crumpled brown-paper sack.

The teacher told me she was really hoping this kid had something to show that the others would appreciate, since she suspected he came from an impoverished background. Sadly, she also told me his parents never came to teacher conferences or school festivities. She had a soft spot for this young man.

To the teacher's dismay, and causing wide eyes from the other kindergartners, the young man pulled out wads and wads of cash totaling $30,000. The bundles were professionally rubber banded into one-thousand-dollar increments. When the teacher excitedly asked him where his treasured show-and-tell item came from, he said, "It belongs to my dad."

Hence the call to the narcotics unit.

It turns out the kid's dad was heavily involved in the distribution of crack cocaine. The Bloods and Crips gangs from Los Angeles had come to Omaha several years earlier to spread their poison, and guys like this father fell into the temptation of easy money and the dangerous lifestyle associated with selling crack cocaine. He was one of many parents born in Omaha who put the priority of selling crack over the welfare of his own kids. I saw it way too often.

I talked to the five-year-old in the presence of the teacher while in the principal's office. I told him he was in no trouble and asked where he found this cash. Without hesitation he told me he was playing in the basement of his house and ran across the cash-stash hidden in one of his larger toys. He told me he didn't check with his dad before he decided to bring the $30,000 cash to school to show his teacher and fellow classmates.

I called my sergeant who instructed me to seize the cash. This was based on the father's previous arrests for selling crack, as well as a vast amount of current intelligence information that he was still active in drug peddling. Our case was further bolstered by the fact the father was unemployed.

However, nothing is as simple as it first appears.

I was still with the five-year-old boy. He had to answer to his drug-dealing dad as to why he brought the $30,000 to show-and-tell. As innocent as this little boy was, I did not want to put him in any danger from his father, or the upper-echelon suppliers who were expecting this money.

This was a sticky situation.

I called the father from the school, identified myself, and told him we had a situation involving his son at the school. I requested he meet me there. I vividly recall having to give him detailed directions on how to drive there, since he had never been to his own son's school.

Once he arrived, I showed him the cash and watched his reaction. His mouth seemed to drop, his breathing escalated, and I asked if he was feeling all right. His son sat nearby, eyes riveted on his father to try to gauge, as much as a five-year-old can, if he was in any sort of trouble.

At first, the dad tried to make excuses for the money, such as selling cars or winning the money while gambling. But I quickly debunked these theories and told him we were not giving the money back to him, and that the Omaha Police would be filing paperwork with the courts to show this money was made from illegal drug sales. I counted the money in front of him, had him sign a receipt, and handed him a copy showing him the money was now in the possession of police.

I watched for any reaction from the dad to his son that would alert me to any danger signs. I saw none. Dad stated he understood the situation, so he was allowed to take his son home. I watched them walk out to the car, with the dad opening the door and his son jumping into the backseat.

For years I have asked myself if that little boy was ever abused.

The unique circumstances of this case gave me no choice but to seize that money and apply for forfeiture proceedings. The father was later indicted and did many years in federal prison. The son's show-and-tell played prominently in his conviction.

I simply could not give this money back to the drug-dealing father. But when I say this case has bothered me for years, I mean it.

6

UNDERCOVER MOM

I n the late 1980s Los Angeles gang members were establishing a foothold in Omaha while selling a poison known as crack cocaine. Conducting business like true entrepreneurs, these cunning and dangerous criminals realized that by infiltrating untapped Midwestern cities like Omaha, Denver, Minneapolis, and Kansas City, they could double or triple their profits from the street price in California.

Neighborhoods in the inner city of Omaha were being taken hostage by newly formed gangs of the Bloods and the Crips who wore red and blue clothing respectively while intimidating law-abiding, decent people who had lived in their modest homes for many years while struggling to raise their children and facing many obstacles along the way.

Crack, a highly addictive form of cocaine, was relatively unknown in Omaha until 1987, when I made my first crack-related arrest in the infamous (and now demolished) Travel Lodge Motel, a spot where the stairwells and elevators smelled like piss during my entire twenty-six-year police career.

The Travel Lodge was located at 39th and Dodge and was one of the seediest roadhouses in Omaha. Three floors of prostitutes, pimps, infidelity, suicides, drug dealing, and general debauchery were all part of the vibe at the Travel Lodge.

Bordered by the historic Joslyn Castle to the north (a real castle, a stone Victorian home to one of the city's founders) and the Blackstone District of Gold Coast mansions to the south, the

Travel Lodge was an eyesore to those who drove by it daily on busy Dodge Street in Omaha.

Travel Lodge Motel, 3900 Dodge Street in Omaha, circa 1960s, home of debauchery and drug dealing.

The sleazy Travel Lodge was not a normal place for upstanding out-of-state visitors to stay while visiting Omaha.

We had received a tip from a snitch about drug activity taking place in a third-floor room. We set up surveillance at night by belly-crawling on a roof of a business across the alley from the motel, which allowed us a clear shot with binoculars to watch what was happening in the suspect's room.

The guy was wearing all red, with huge gold chains around his neck. We were not accustomed to seeing this type of apparel, and judging by the constant short-term foot traffic to and from the room, we knew we were onto something.

After all, we were trained to watch for certain characteristics indicative of drug dealing at hotels and motels. Lots of foot traffic, short visits, excessive phone calls, people parking a block away and walking to the room, and not allowing maids to clean the room were but a few red flags that led us to believe nefarious activity was taking place.

We also had officers in undercover vehicles stationed around the Travel Lodge, ready to follow suspicious cars after the occupants left the motel room. Running the license plates gave us vital intelligence information about the people the guy in the room was selling drugs to or, more importantly, receiving his drug stash from.

THAT DAMN FOURTH AMENDMENT

We decided to stop one guy after he left the room. Surveillance officers on the roof across from the room saw a classic drug deal take place. The customer was a black male in his teens, and when he entered the motel room, the kid immediately handed something to the guy in the room. The dealer opened a dresser drawer, retrieved what looked like a plastic baggie, and handed it to the kid who closely examined it before putting the baggie in his right front pocket.

Over the police radio a good description was transmitted of the customer as he left the room. He walked out a side door of the motel to a waiting piece of junk Chevrolet Impala, driven by a young girl.

Minutes later, at my request, a marked Omaha Police cruiser stopped the Impala a half-mile away after observing the female driver fail to signal her intent to make a righthand turn. Probable cause was needed for the suspect car to be pulled over. If we had no valid reason to detain the car and occupants, the whole investigation might be thrown out later in court based on violations of the Fourth Amendment of the Bill of Rights, which guards against unreasonable search and seizure.

I remember backing up the uniformed officers on the traffic stop. Being assigned to the narcotics unit, I drove an undercover car and dressed in blue jeans and T-shirts. I usually parked my car away from scenes like this traffic stop to prevent my car from being burned on future investigations.

The kid who had bought the drugs from the motel room was nervous, especially when he saw narcotics unit officers approaching him at the scene of the traffic stop. I told him to assume a position on the car so I could pat him down for weapons. As I did so, I felt the plastic baggie in his pants pocket containing something hard, though I couldn't make out what it was. Since I could not articulate that the object in his pants was a weapon, it was illegal for me to remove it.

That damn Fourth Amendment really posed some challenges. I doubt when James Madison and his buddies wrote the landmark legislation in the late 1700s, worried about British soldiers rampaging through citizens' houses in the newly formed United States of America, that they could have ever envisioned police officers dealing with gangs, drugs, and high-powered weapons two hundred years later.

No matter my opinion, we still had to conduct ourselves lawfully on traffic stops such as this. So my next step was to simply ask the kid if he had any drugs on him.

"No" was his response.

"Well then," I retorted, "do you mind if I check your pockets just to make sure?"

He paused, with a panicked look on his face. But like most drug dealers put in that situation, he realized the jig was up, and the look of resignation on his face told me bad things were in store for this kid.

"Yeah, man, go ahead," he said, head hung low.

The concept of the consensual search is perfectly legal, as long as police officers do not intimidate or coerce the suspect into granting police officers permission to search their person, car, or house. It was common for bad guys to allow police officers to search without a warrant, even knowing they were certainly going to prison for what the cop was going to find.

I carefully reached into his right front pants pockets. Cops are trained to be cautious when searching people. Needles and razor blades, both tools of the drug-dealing trade, pose immense danger to police officers' health and well-being. No cop wants to take hepatitis B or C or HIV home to their family.

I pulled the baggie out of his pants pocket and noticed a golf-ball-sized rock, yellowish-white in color, that I did not recognize. I had been an Omaha Police officer for ten years at this point and thought I was streetwise.

I had also heard of crack cocaine and how potent and dangerous it was. We had been briefed that crack was on its way to Omaha, though we had no timetable as to when it would be on the streets.

Now we knew.

This was the first significant seizure of crack cocaine in Omaha, Nebraska.

We arrested both occupants of the Impala and got them and the car out of the area as quickly as possible so as not to alert the dealer in the nearby motel room.

Within several hours of the traffic stop, we had a signed search warrant for the third-floor motel room. Of significance was that the warrant was labeled a no-knock, meaning we could enter the room by using a battering ram to break down the door. No-knock search warrants were allowed if officers could articulate to the judge that, if they were required to knock on the door and announce who they were, the evidence being sought could be destroyed by flushing it down a toilet or sink.

In this situation, the size of the ball of crack we seized from the kid on the traffic stop could flush very easily. Any other crack cocaine in the room could quickly be destroyed if the dealer knew we were coming.

As I led a team quietly down the hallway to the dealer's room, two of the stronger officers held a seventy-five-pound battering ram that was powerful enough to knock the motel room door off its hinges with one swing.

And that is exactly what happened.

Within seconds the door flew open and officers flooded the room. The suspect in all red was standing by the window, and, without any thought for his safety, he leaped through the window and fell twenty feet to the alley below where several officers were stationed. The suspect sustained a severe fracture of his ankle and was writhing in pain as I looked out the third-floor window in amazement to the scene below.

Crack cocaine seized during 1991 Omaha drug raid.

This was a good search warrant. We located additional amounts of crack cocaine in the room, along with bundles of cash, a handgun, and a beeper that would not stop going off.

Most interesting was the home city on the driver's license of the guy with the broken ankle: Inglewood, California. We all looked at each other as if to say, "Get ready, boys, things are changing in Omaha, Nebraska!"

THE CALIFORNIA CRACK CONNECTION: 1987

Several months later, and after many hours of surveillance, interviews, conversations with Los Angeles police detectives, examination of airline flight information, and good basic detective work, we identified an Omaha native as being one of the main conduits between California crack connections and the ripe, fertile customer base growing in numbers by the day in Omaha.

A star athlete in high school, and standing at least 6 foot 5, "Paul" was an imposing figure who was well known in the poverty-stricken areas of Omaha. It did not go unnoticed by both the police and Paul's family and friends that beginning in the late 1980s Paul's standard of living greatly improved.

He was driving a fancy Jeep with a removable top, sporting thick tires and a sound system heard from blocks away. His was one of the few vehicles with an installed cellular telephone, which drew stares and comments as he drove down the streets of North Omaha showing off his new toys.

Keep in mind this was 1987. Cell phones were far from common.

Paul enjoyed the good life and especially showing others around him the overnight success he had achieved.

We determined that Paul was a major target and that a large contingent of narcotics unit officers would be devoted to putting him out of business. We began by organizing surveillances on him, his vehicle, and his apartment.

A court order was obtained that authorized a pen-register to be placed on his home phone and cell phone. A pen-register—also known as a dialed number recorder—is an electronic device that records all numbers called from a telephone line. We worked with the local telephone company's security team that electronically activated the device once we presented them the court order.

We found out that Paul was calling numerous Los Angeles–area numbers. Several stood out as being called more often. In working with LAPD detectives, we identified Paul's main co-conspirators that he was working with to bring multiple pounds of cocaine into Omaha. These were California gang members well known to the LAPD.

I was impressed with how cooperative the Los Angeles detectives were with us. They were quick to share information, drive by addresses in Los Angeles at our request to see if Nebraska plated cars were present, and fly to Omaha to testify on the cases we were building. It was a true cooperative effort.

Paul posed challenges to the surveillance officers assigned to monitor his every move. He drove like a bat out of hell, navigating at high speeds while weaving in and out of traffic like a mad man. He may have been doing this to thwart surveillance by law enforcement since drug dealers are paranoid by nature. Or being a pathological criminal, he may simply have thought he was above the law when it came to his driving and the safety of those innocent civilians around him.

He was seen yakking on his cell phone at the same time, which did not go unnoticed by the surveillance officers.

Cell phones were a novelty, and the fact that Paul had one certainly added to his aura. Our plan was to gather enough evidence to obtain a wiretap order so that we could hear who he was talking to and what he and the co-conspirators were planning, rather than simply trying to guess after correlating the pen-register data coupled with the surveillances.

Wiretaps on cellular phones were in the early stages by 1987. We were confident that the Omaha Police Department, partnering with the FBI, could handle this complex investigative technique.

Wiretaps were the ultimate investigative tool to take down a drug operation. Before a judge would sign an order authorizing a wiretap, we had to exhaust all investigative efforts, especially surveillance. The judge would only sign the wiretap order if he or she determined the wiretap was the last-ditch effort to bring down the organization.

The one problem we had was the location of Paul's apartment. Located in the west end of a large apartment complex in central Omaha, Paul had picked the perfect location to thwart any type of police surveillance. His top floor apartment looked out over the entire parking lot, so any attempts to park an undercover officer in an unmarked car or nondescript van may well have been undermined by Paul or his henchmen. Snitches told us that Paul was constantly on the lookout for cops watching him.

If only we could hide ourselves in an apartment overlooking Paul's.

This is where the case became bizarre.

THE PERFECT SETUP

My dear mother, Elizabeth, had been living in an apartment in Paul's complex for several years. Coincidentally, Mom's apartment afforded a clear view into Paul's living room as well as the portion of the parking lot where he parked his car. From my mom's living room, we could see who was coming and going and how long they stayed.

It was a perfect setup.

I will never forget going to my mom's apartment and explaining to her about the investigation and who was involved. Before I finished the first few sentences, my mom said, "I bet you're going to tell me about the guy in the top-floor apartment over there," pointing to Paul's place.

I was not surprised at all. My mom was always sharp as a tack and had street-sense about her. After all, she had been married to a US Marshal for over forty years.

She knew the comings and goings of most of her neighbors, from the cop in the ground floor apartment whose patio was a revolving door for women, to the couple who lived one building over who had alcohol-fueled yelling matches on a regular basis. In the summer, Mom knew what the arguments were about.

Mom had noticed lots of activity coming and going from Paul's apartment and was not surprised that his apartment was a hub for a large-scale crack cocaine operation. She readily volunteered her apartment to be used for a surveillance point.

I was not so sure. I certainly did not want to place my mom in any danger. She lived alone and was in her seventies. I continually asked myself if this was a good idea.

But the newly installed wiretap on Paul's cell phone was providing us helpful information. We knew that a major load of cocaine was due to arrive in the next week and most certainly would be taken straight to his apartment. Paul was not being careful what he said on his phone.

Mom's apartment could be a valuable resource in bringing down the organization. So I agreed to allow her apartment to be used under one condition: Paul must never know we used Mom's apartment for surveillance. Any probable cause for his arrest, or for others in the organization, had to be developed independent of what we saw from my mom's apartment. I could not put Mom in a position to be named in police reports or to be required to testify.

We all agreed, including my mom, on the parameters.

THE EAGLE'S NEST GOES INTO OPERATION

Within hours Mom's apartment was dubbed the Eagle's Nest—code for the primary surveillance position being used to assist us in determining when the load of cocaine would arrive in Omaha from California before being taken to Paul's apartment.

For three full days, around the clock, the Eagle's Nest was manned. I was a bit worried how Mom would react to all the manpower and equipment in her living room.

She did not disappoint.

The living room of her apartment was truly an amazing sight. A high-powered telescope was in place, aimed directly into Paul's living room. Police communication equipment was strewn everywhere, along with cameras on tripods. Cops were assigned to eight-hour shifts and flipped coins on who would be lucky enough to be with my mom. She made them unbelievable meals and desserts and knew all the officers by name.

My mom was in her glory. She was right in the middle of the activity, while making sure she was not a hindrance.

The only rule Mom was given was no outsiders were allowed in her apartment. Her group of friends, all the same age, could not know what was going on for fear of blabbing to the wrong person. It was tough to keep a low profile about what Mom's apartment was being used for, but she did. She realized that Paul and his group were dangerous people who needed to be taken off the street.

I was proud of her.

Toward the end of the third day, the phone call finally came in over the wiretap. Paul's wife was going to smuggle a pound of cocaine on a flight from Los Angeles to Omaha, arriving around 11:00 p.m. She would then take a cab to Paul's apartment where they would immediately begin the process of distributing the cocaine out on the streets to their people.

This operation was taking place over a dozen years prior to September 11, 2001, the dark day when terrorists commandeered planes to take down the World Trade Center. Prior to that day, drugs were frequently smuggled into Omaha on planes, hidden in luggage, diaper bags, or body carried by the courier. After 9/11, security was increased at airports so severely that drug interdictions at airports (including Omaha's) all but ceased.

Paul realized the longer the pound of cocaine stayed in his apartment, the better his chances of being arrested. Therefore, as cops, we knew we had a short window of opportunity to take down Paul and his wife.

The timing of their arrests would be determined by what was seen by officers in the Eagle's Nest.

The plane from LA arrived on time, and we saw Paul's wife depart with simply a carry-on bag. She had not checked any luggage, which was common for drug couriers. She wanted to get out of the airport to the awaiting cab as quickly as possible.

I was one of the surveillance officers and saw her hail a cab outside of Omaha's Eppley Airfield. We followed the cab to the general area of Paul's apartment. Because of the officers in the Eagle's Nest (Mom's apartment), the ground units broke off the cab several blocks away from Paul's place. There was no need for us to get burned this late in the investigation.

The surveillance cameras in Mom's apartment were placed behind the partially opened blinds in her living room. The officers were careful not to be noticed while in her apartment, across the parking lot from Paul's apartment.

Officers in the Eagle's Nest called out, "The cab has arrived, and the target has exited."

Several minutes later we heard over our radios, "Target is now in the apartment. She and her husband are looking in the carry-on bag in the dining room." I was surprised that Paul did not do a better job of closing his curtains, especially during the drug deals taking place. I assumed he felt comfortable with his upper-floor apartment being safe from surveillance.

Within minutes Paul was making calls on his cell phone, telling his people to come to his apartment right away.

We had to act immediately.

SIGNAL 88

Our raid team ascended the steps to Paul's top-floor apartment. I remembered thinking to myself that my mom was listening to me on the radio, knowing I was going to rush into this drug dealer's apartment in just seconds.

I had second thoughts about involving my mother in this crazy scenario. How worried she must have been. What if shots were fired when we rushed in? What if I was shot, or one of the officers she had just become acquainted with?

These thoughts went through my mind as we approached Paul's door, but it was too late to turn back. We bashed the door with a battering ram, yelled "POLICE, GET DOWN," and quickly swept through the two-bedroom apartment.

We found Paul and his wife in a back bedroom with a pound of fresh cocaine lying on the bed.

I said into the radio, "We are signal 88," meaning all officers were safe. I wanted my mom to know this as soon as possible.

Within minutes the Eagle's Nest ceased to exist. All the equipment was removed, and Mom's life returned to normal. Paul never had a clue that Omaha Police were less than fifty yards away from his apartment, watching him through a high-powered telescope, while listening to his phone calls.

Mom's friends were never told that across the hall from their quiet existence was the hub of a major narcotics surveillance concentrating on a large-scale cocaine operation doing business right under their noses.

Numerous individuals (including Paul and his wife) were federally indicted in the case and served lengthy prison sentences.

My mom was a strong woman and never hesitated to assist us in this investigation. Would I ask her again? Probably not. But if I did, I'm confident what her answer would be.

7

COCAINE, COP KILLERS, AND CRIPS

The Greyhound pulled into the Omaha bus depot downtown in the early morning, having traveled through flat Nebraska overnight from Denver and points west.

Maybe the traveler was transferring in Omaha to a Chicago-bound bus or to Detroit or something south, maybe to Kansas City. Maybe Omaha was his destination. But when the tired passengers staggered off the bus, his suitcase vanished.

Within hours of the disappearance of the suitcase, the streets were abuzz with activity over a windfall of white powder. Cocaine. Snitches told us there was a scurry among those who had the ten kilos to hide the stash and to quickly start selling off the cocaine.

We found its contents—twenty-two pounds (ten kilos) of cocaine, wrapped in duct tape—on the streets of Omaha.

It was March 1989. The street value of the lost shipment: $1.2 million.

Whether the traveler was a delivery man for the LA gangs, we never knew. And whether the thief knew of the valuable and dangerous contents, we never found out.

One homeless guy found four bricks of the stolen cocaine in an alley near the bus station. He was sober enough to realize that he wanted nothing to do with this, so he quickly called 911 and turned over his discovery.

We found four more kilos of cocaine hidden in the suspended ceiling of an apartment laundry room, several blocks to the west of the bus station. Two more kilos of cocaine were found hidden in an attic of a house in the North Omaha area.

Within several hours of the suitcase being stolen, we had recovered most if not all the kilos of cocaine, before it could be sold. Our confidential street informants had done well and received a handsome payday for their vital information.

Sgt. Bill Agnew of the Omaha Police Department narcotics unit was quoted in the *Omaha World-Herald* as saying, "The ten kilos seized so far appear to be the result of foiled transportation at the bus depot."

Somebody had to answer for losing all that cocaine. I'm sure that was a tough conversation. And the conversation was potentially with the street gangs that had invaded Omaha.

By 1989 the Bloods and the Crips gangs from Los Angeles were well established here. Gang members realized the profitability found on the streets of Omaha, where they could double the prices they were charging in California due to a new and emerging customer base who had never before tasted the poison known as crack cocaine.

In fact, when the gangs first started selling crack in Omaha in 1987, they did so at dirt cheap prices in order to hook the customer base. The smokers were easily addicted, and the prices then began a systematic increase.

Millions of dollars in crack cocaine sales were generated yearly, verified by the large amounts of cash being seized along with the analyzation of Western Union money orders being wired daily by the Omaha dealers to the top-echelon gang members in the Los Angeles area.

Suburbs like Inglewood, California, sent Crenshaw Mafia Gangsters to Omaha. Compton, California, produced the Piru gang, which was also well represented. This is only to name a few of the subsets of Bloods and Crips gang members in Omaha in 1989.

The Omaha Police began seizing amounts of cocaine and crack cocaine never dreamed of a few years earlier. Along with the increased amounts of cocaine came the escalating threats of violence to Omaha Police officers.

Los Angeles gang members arrested during crack raid in Omaha, 1988 with faces obscured.

From California, the Bloods and Crips brought with them a culture of brotherhood, loyalty, and fierceness. The Omaha Police Department saw an escalation in drive-by shootings, as well as the seriousness of the caliber of weapons being seized. AK-47s, Mini .223 assault rifles, and semiautomatic handguns with high-capacity magazines became the rage.

We served no-knock search warrant after no-knock search warrant in high-crime areas. Frequently we heard high-pitched whistling all around the drug house we had hit, which was the universal signal that *one-time* (street slang for the police) was in the area.

The term *one-time* for police officers was popularized in the 1990s by the Los Angeles gangs. The meaning is, "You can fuck with me one time, and after that I will shoot your motherfucking ass."

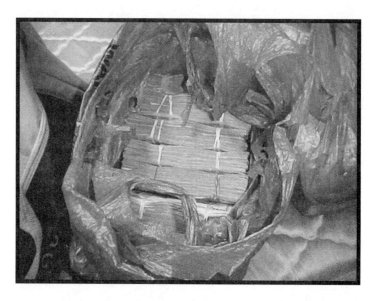

$300,000 cash seized during 1991 crack cocaine raid in Omaha.

At times we would hear a rapid-fire succession of shots within several blocks of where we were, meant to intimidate us and send a message that the gangs were not scared of us.

In 1992 we served a search warrant with the Emergency Response Unit (SWAT team) at a house near 18th and Ohio, in North Omaha. This was one of many crack warrants executed over the years in this impoverished neighborhood, permeated by boarded-up houses and vacant lots filled with trash.

My practice was to post police officers around the perimeter of the scene for security purposes. Black-and-white police cruisers were clearly visible in front of the houses we were searching, with officers standing in the front and back. This was done to protect my narcotics officers who were busy searching the house as well as vehicles and outbuildings in the yard.

I made sure the neighborhood understood an army of police officers was in the hood and that, while we conducted our search of the target house, we were totally in charge of that area.

I was standing in the front yard with SWAT command officers when suddenly the cold, crisp night air was shattered by a hail of gunfire from a large-caliber rifle. The shots were coming from less than a block away, and branches directly above our heads were snapping from the rapid-fire rounds being fired.

I remember dropping to the dirt in the front yard, and with the others we tried to find any type of cover that could protect us. The shots were over in seconds, and quickly we fanned out to try to find the shooter.

The culprit was elusive and quick, and he was never found.

I was quoted in the paper the following day as saying, "If it was meant for intimidation purposes the motive failed, because it did not intimidate us." Actually, I was scared shitless. The war was on, and our enemy had a distinct advantage.

The Bloods and Crips had the mentality that, eventually, their criminal way of thinking was going to catch up to them. Many told me they would be dead by the age of twenty-one. They told me they didn't expect a long life, so they were going to cause as much chaos as possible in the time they had.

They had nothing to lose.

To add to the concern of police officers nationwide were the lyrics by rapper Ice-T for a song titled "Cop Killer." Released by the group Body Count on the 1992 album *Body Count*, the lyrics sent a chill up my spine the first time I heard them. You can imagine the message about killing cops and police brutality and getting even.

Why in God's name was a song like this ever recorded? It was an overnight sensation. Upon the release of the song, I overheard crowds of onlookers rapping the lyrics at outdoor crime scenes where we were arresting suspects for selling crack.

Ice-T defended his lyrics, stating, "I'm singing in the first person as a character who is fed up with police brutality. I ain't never killed no cop. I felt like it a lot of times. But I never did it."

"Cop Killer" was heavily criticized by President George H. W. Bush, as well as by national police organizations. Pro-law enforcement groups demanded the song's withdrawal from commercial availability, citing concerns of promoting anti-police sentiment.

Eventually, Ice-T caved in and took the song off the album, though it was still available for purchase as a single. But by that time, the damage had been done. The hateful, dangerous message sent through the lyrics—which I will not print here—further created the culture of violence by dangerous gang members toward police officers.

On August 20, 1995, Omaha Police Officer Jimmy Wilson Jr. was murdered while sitting in his police cruiser by a gang member armed with a high-powered assault rifle. Wilson still had his seat belt on, and his gun was holstered.

On September 11, 2003, Omaha Police Sergeant Jason Pratt was ambushed by a hard-core gang member. The suspect had just run from a traffic stop. He then leaped from some bushes and shot Sergeant Pratt while he was searching the area. Pratt died days later.

On May 20, 2015, Omaha Police Officer Kerrie Orozco was shot and killed by a gang member whom she was chasing through backyards. Orozco was due to go on maternity leave the following day to take her daughter, born prematurely several months before, home from the hospital for the first time.

APPLAUSE ACCOMPANIES DRUG ARRESTS

Residents near 24th Street and Larimore Avenue applauded Wednesday night as narcotics officers toted away several Omahans during an undercover drug operation.

Sgt. Mark Langan said officers began watching the area about 9 p.m. after receiving numerous complaints about drug activity in the neighborhood.

"In the past several years, the area has been a heavy open-air crack (cocaine) market," Langan said. "There were several complaints that it had started again. We want the neighbors to know that we haven't forgotten about them and we'll continue to monitor the area."

During the operation, police saw an 18-year-old Omaha man arrive in a 1979 Chevrolet Malibu. Langan said the man then began distributing crack cocaine to people in the area.

"As officers began converging on the man, he threw a plastic baggie with 10 pieces of crack cocaine," Langan said. The man was taken into custody and booked on suspicion of delivery of crack cocaine and possession of crack cocaine with intent to deliver.

Langan said the 18-year-old was arrested in a drug-free school zone, about 870 feet from Saratoga School, 2504 Meredith Avenue. Federal law provides double the penalty if a person is convicted of selling or using drugs within 1,000 feet of a school.

Omaha World-Herald, July 18, 1990

Reprinted with permission of the *Omaha World-Herald*.

Ice-T's song laid the foundation for hatred toward police officers by drug dealing and murderous gang members, both in Omaha and nationwide.

Letter and illustrated envelope seized from
a jail inmate in Omaha, Nebraska, in 1991.

Let me be clear. We had support from many neighbors in these high-crime areas. Some were prisoners in their own homes, held hostage by the armed gang members who were slinging crack on the streets in front of them. Most of that support was silent, for fear of retaliation.

I despise Ice-T's song "Cop Killer."

So what happened to Ice-T after the dust settled from "Cop Killer" and he decided to move on with his career?

Since 2000 he has portrayed a police officer on the hit show *Law & Order: SVU*. Think about that. He rapped about killing cops, and now he plays one on television. Where does his loyalty lie? Perhaps in the almighty buck. His net worth is estimated to be $40 million.

Only in America!

8

EVEN THIS JESUS
CAN'T SAVE YOU

It seems there is a patron saint for just about everything. The patron saint for police officers is Saint Michael. The patron saint for firefighters is Saint Florian.

And the patron saint for drug dealers is "Saint" Jesús Malverde.

Say what?

Jesús Malverde, known as the narco-saint, is a folklore hero in the Mexican state of Sinaloa—regarded as one of the main regions responsible for cocaine and methamphetamine smuggling by the Sinaloa cartel into the United States.

This Jesús is celebrated as a folk saint by some in Mexico and in the United States, particularly among drug traffickers. It was not uncommon for us to find shrines of Jesús Malverde in houses, apartments, and hotel rooms. The adorations were impressive, complete with statues, lit candles, and medallions depicting the good saint.

A shrine to Jesús Malverde meant the drugs and money were not too far away.

We found pictures of Malverde stuffed in kilos of methamphetamine or cocaine, or with bundles of cash ready to be sent back to cartel lords in Sinaloa.

The pics were considered good luck charms to provide some type of divine protection for the stashes of drugs and cash.

Interdiction officers on Interstate 80, which traverses the country through the heart of Omaha, frequently found statues and prayer cards for Jesús Malverde on the dashboards of cars traveling from California. Soon the officers located pounds of methamphetamine or cocaine in the gas tanks or hidden compartments.

Shrine to Jesús Malverde, similar to many found in Omaha homes during drug raids.

Several times we placed drug dealers into our police cars after they were arrested. Within seconds they were heard praying in Spanish to Malverde, imploring him to save them from incarceration, and for us to not find the dope. They failed to realize that the blond, pale-skinned officer sitting with them understood their emotional plea.

Joaquín Guzman, aka El Chapo, was the notorious head of the Sinaloa drug cartel until his arrest by US law enforcement in 2017. His team of high-paid lawyers were praying they could get the notorious accused drug lord acquitted, and they turned to Mexico's narco-saint Malverde for help.

A six-inch statuette of the folk hero, who is hailed in El Chapo's home country as an "angel of the poor," was prominently featured on a shelf inside the defense's conference room in Brooklyn federal court.

Even Malverde could not save El Chapo, who was found guilty on all counts and sentenced in July 2019 to life in prison plus thirty years. He was ordered to forfeit more than $12.6 billion.

El Chapo is now serving his sentence at the federal supermax prison in Florence, Colorado.

Maybe he has a shrine to Jesús Malverde in his cell.

9

DON'T CALL HER BABY MAMA

During my law enforcement career, certain street terms grated on me like fingernails on a chalkboard.

First, my name wasn't *dude*. I quickly reminded arrestees to refer to me as Sir or Sergeant Langan.

Referring to their wife or girlfriend as the *old lady* always brought a quick retort from me, while pointing out they were lucky to have such females who were willing to associate with their own pathetic selves. In fact, when I was dating my wife, she made it clear it was unacceptable to refer to any significant other as the old lady, especially her.

But the one that really got under my skin was the offensive, demeaning term *baby mama*. This phrase was frequently used by drug dealers we arrested to describe the young, immature girlfriend who, because of self-esteem issues and drug addictions, birthed a baby that neither she nor the piece of crap father was ready to nurture, love, and provide for.

Drug dealers routinely take advantage of dependent girls who have never had parental support in their young lives. These girls are impressionable and easily enamored by the free-wheeling, money-throwing young men who swoop into their lives, promising them that they are the only ones who matter to them. The deal is quickly sealed between the two, resulting in a baby being born into a world that provides little chance for success.

It's not uncommon for a young male criminal to have babies with multiple baby mamas. I have seen this scenario over and over, and I always ask myself, "Why not just use a condom?"

"THIS AIN'T MY BABY"

In the early 1990s my narcotics unit crew did a no-knock search warrant in the crime-infested Pleasant View housing projects in North Omaha. This area was a hub of crack cocaine activity, and we did hundreds of similar search warrants trying to stem the flow of this dangerous drug.

No-knock search warrants allow police officers to conduct a forcible entry into an address. Many search warrants looking for items such as stolen televisions or stolen car parts require officers to stand outside the front door and yell "police officers, search warrant, we demand entry."

But if we drug cops could convince a judge that the evidence being sought such as crack cocaine could easily be destroyed (by flushing it down a sink or toilet), we are authorized to take a battering ram to the door, bust it down, and race into the house before the suspected dealers inside can do anything to eradicate the evidence.

Another reason for a no-knock search warrant was the presence of weapons in the house that could be used to shoot us if we gave the bad guys enough advance warning that we were coming in.

I always referred to no-knock search warrant entries as controlled chaos. We were all well briefed on what our job duties were during these dynamic entries. But when the door flew open, suspects were running to the back of the house, ditching drugs, and throwing guns. Dogs were trying to bite us.

It was total bedlam.

The Pleasant View housing area was one of numerous complexes operated by the Omaha Housing Authority. Unaffectionately referred to as the projects or the jets, these units provided low-income and subsidized housing for thousands of dependent citizens.

On the flipside, these areas were attractive locations for crack cocaine sales and gang activity. Besides Pleasant View there were the Hilltop, Spencer, Logan Fontenelle, and South Side housing areas, each with their own gang identity and subsequent problems such as open-air drug dealing, drive-by shootings, and homicides.

I was struck by the sense of a lack of hope among many of the residents living in these nondescript, tenement-style housing units.

These project units, spread across both North and South Omaha, were parts of the city never seen by most Omaha citizens who lived only a few miles away. Yet the two sides seemed to be thousands of miles apart in many areas including economic status, schools, and a general sense of lifestyle.

The no-knock entry we did in the Pleasant View housing area was on a sunny midweek afternoon.

We knew through informant information that a large-scale drug dealer was using a woman's apartment to stash crack cocaine. This was common, as the dealers wanted a layer of security between them and the goods. But they had to pick a spot where their property was safe. In the dealer's mind, this unit provided a haven for his cache of drugs.

We ran up to the heavy, solid wooden door protected by a fortified metal frame. The doors of the units in the low-income Pleasant View apartments required a two-man ram—meaning I picked two of my stronger officers to man the seventy-five-pound piece of steel, shaped like a five-foot-long cylinder, with handles on both sides. The cardinal rule of the ram officers was not to drop the ram on their partner's foot once the door was breached. That was a guaranteed trip to the hospital.

After several whacks, the door flung open, and we rushed in to find a young woman with a newborn baby on the sofa. The unit was sparsely furnished. The twenty-something female was sitting on the only furniture in the living room.

The baby was lying on her back, thankfully oblivious to the dramatic scene taking place around her.

The kitchen had piles of dirty plates in the sink, with baby formula and bottles on the countertop.

The upstairs bedroom consisted of only a mattress on the floor with soiled linens and blankets. There was a small television at the foot of the bed propped on top of a cardboard shelving unit. Next to the bed was a plate with drug paraphernalia, marijuana residue, and a glass crack pipe.

Under a dirty pile of clothes in the closet we found the stash of crack cocaine left by the dealer for this young lady to watch over while at the same time trying to tend to the needs of the weeks-old baby girl.

It was a sad scene.

She was defiant and scared at the same time. She knew she was in trouble as soon as we found the dealer's stash of crack cocaine in an upstairs closet. But she also knew she was in hot water with her dealer-boyfriend, who was now out of thousands of dollars of revenue.

After the crack was found, I said to her, "You're under arrest for possessing crack cocaine with the intent to deliver." I then handcuffed her, had a female officer search her, and she was allowed to sit back down next to the baby.

Next, I uttered a line that has resounded with me for years, especially considering the answer she gave me.

"Since you're under arrest, I'm going to place your baby in foster care."

"This ain't my baby, it's my grandbaby!" she yelled back, appearing offended that I assumed this twenty-seven-year-old, soon-to-be-convicted drug dealer was anything but this baby's mother.

Think about this scenario. The cycle of young teen girls having babies, and their own young teen girls repeating the cycle, is part of many systemic issues plaguing the inner city of large municipalities around the United States. Poverty, lack of parenting, drugs, and gang activity have contributed to the phenomenon known as babies having babies.

How many babies might have been birthed by now by the newborn baby girl found on that sofa in the Pleasant View projects in the early 1990s? She might likely already be a grandmother herself.

Do the math.

10

THE DIRTY DIAPER AND THE DRUG-DEALING DEN

I consider myself a glass is half-full type of guy.

Sure, there were days in my police career when I came home and thought civilization as we knew it was coming to an end. This was based on the terrible things I saw and the horrendous human beings I dealt with.

But I have always realized how lucky I am to have grown up in a supportive household, and to marry a great gal who gave us two kids who make us proud every day.

Many of us presume the joys in our lives. However, grandkids are the best and must never be taken for granted. Over the past nine years I have been revitalized with the additions of Colin and Drew to our family table.

Grandkids are like dogs (sorry to Colin and Drew for the analogy). Their love is never-ending, probably because we spoil them rotten every chance we get. And, like dogs, they are always looking to see where we are and what we're doing, while at the same time wanting that safe and secure feeling that they are loved and protected.

And grandkids and dogs are always scouring for snacks! You would think they were never fed.

Grandkids are the most sacred possession for any grandparent. Nothing compares.

Which brings me to Paula, a wretched excuse of a woman who placed the almighty methamphetamine over the welfare of herself, her adult child, and even her own granddaughter.

We arrested Paula in May 2001 after we served a search warrant at her house in midtown Omaha. We had obtained the search warrant to hit her house after confidential informants told us of the drug dealing taking place from the residence.

Paula was in her middle forties and had the look of what we characterized as a tweaker—a hard-core methamphetamine user. She was skinny and gaunt, with scraggly hair that hadn't been combed in days.

Paula was wearing a black tank top that exposed tattoos on her right breast. Hygiene is not a priority for tweakers, and many times I could smell their dirty hair and unclean clothes.

The worst part of dealing with tweakers was their breath. Consider the fact that meth is made using chemicals such as sulfuric acid, drain cleaner, and antifreeze. The term *meth mouth* refers to a user's teeth rotting away along with their gums and taste buds. The stench emitting from their mouths was unbearable at times.

The house was a mess with junk and crap strewn throughout, with dirty dishes both in the living room and in the kitchen sink.

Located during the search were four ounces of methamphetamine, a scale used to weigh drugs, and $1,000 cash. Four ounces was definitely a dealer amount and would sell for as much as $8,000 on the streets if broken down into smaller amounts.

We also found some drug records denoting first names and dollar amounts owed. This was not uncommon as the drug dealers needed a way to keep track of money in and money out.

There was nothing out of the ordinary for this investigation. We literally had conducted hundreds like it. But there was one glaring difference inside Paula's drug-dealing den.

Her granddaughter, not quite a year old, was lying on the bed of Paula's bedroom. It was obvious this poor little girl had severe physical and neurological disabilities, and my heart sank when I saw her. There was medical equipment throughout the bedroom that assisted the little girl to breathe, eat, and survive. She appeared to be noncommunicative and obviously required round-the-clock care to sustain her life.

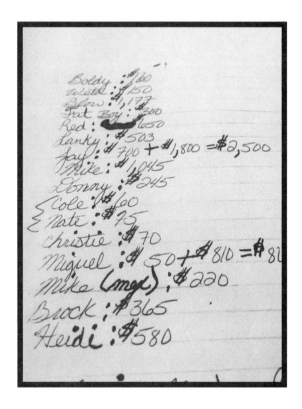

Drug records seized from Paula's house in a bust.

Paula's nineteen-year-old daughter was also in the house. She was the mother of this poor child, and the thought immediately entered my mind as to whether, based on the daughter's tweaker appearance, this poor little baby's disabilities were based on methamphetamine use during the pregnancy.

It was also sad that most of the drugs and associated paraphernalia located in this house were in the same bedroom as this baby, who had no clue what was going on around her.

In true fashion Paula ratted out her boyfriend as being the main kingpin of the operation. According to Paula, her boyfriend Chico was receiving quarter-pound amounts of meth from his nephew on a regular basis.

Paula stated she was being "forced" by Chico to sell methamphetamine for him and that she was also a user of the drug.

Sadly, Chico had left prior to us hitting the house, but according to Paula he was meeting his nephew to get more methamphetamine. She did not know where and when the meet was occurring, but she did give us a good description of Chico as being a Mexican man about thirty-six years old, with black hair. She gave us his cell phone number and a description of his red pickup truck.

We waited for over an hour for Chico to return but he never did. Perhaps he saw us hit the house, or when he came back, he saw police cars parked in front of his house. Whatever the situation, I was worried we would never find Chico.

Paula was arrested and booked for possession of methamphetamine to deliver. Her daughter, the mother of Paula's disabled granddaughter, was left to care for the child.

Days passed and my crew then moved on to new cases, forgetting about Paula and Chico.

Fast-forward about five months to September 21, 2001. Just ten days after 9/11 and the attacks on the World Trade Center, the country was still reeling from the huge loss of life we all endured. What a terrible tragedy that was.

However, there were still drug dealers to arrest in Omaha, Nebraska, and my crew was working the afternoon shift as normal.

That night we received a tip from a person we had just arrested that Paula and Chico were back selling drugs at a house in South Omaha. Paula was on bond for the drug raid at her house back in May, and Chico had still not been located. I wanted to act as quickly as we could because I really wanted to take Chico into custody and get him off the streets.

Luckily, we located Chico in the yard of a house nearby the address the informant had told us about. When we arrested him, he had more methamphetamine on his person, which didn't surprise me.

We then approached the house where Paula was supposedly selling from. We did not have time to obtain a search warrant because I feared Paula knew we were onto her. So I took a team of six officers to the front door and knocked. Luckily, Paula was close to the door, and she allowed us into the house.

Present in this 987-square-foot house were thirteen people. To say they were crammed into the house is an understatement.

People and kids were everywhere, but one stood out from the pack. Lying on the couch, surrounded by people and booze, was the now one-year-old severely disabled granddaughter that we had first met in May at Paula's other house.

Her grave situation had not improved, and the poor baby made periodic gasping noises as her method of breathing to stay alive. At one point she vomited, evoking an immediate response from Paula. I assured Paula that while we were there, she could tend to the baby's needs.

Paula was nervous yet cooperative. She assured me no drugs were present in the house, and she actually gave us permission to look around. She sat by her disabled granddaughter in the living room while we inspected the house.

Shortly after the search began, one of my narcotics officers approached me with a serious look on his face.

"Sarge," he said, "I just saw Paula stick something down the baby's diaper."

Oh shit, I thought. How are we going to handle this?

I had experienced piece-of-shit drug dealers using kids to hide drugs before. Whether in their car seats or hidden inside their toys in the kids' bedroom, I knew that drug dealers had no loyalty to their kids when it came to staying out of jail.

But this was a sticky situation, since the child in question was severely disabled and the officer was unsure what Paula had stuck down the diaper.

Was she simply checking the diaper for a mess? Had she shoved a gun down there, which posed a risk to everybody in the house?

I asked Paula to come back to her bedroom where I spoke to her with another officer. I also asked her to carry her disabled granddaughter with her.

"Paula, we think you may have hidden something in the baby's diaper," I said.

She became upset and began crying, denying the allegations. "How dare you say I would hide drugs on my granddaughter. Just look at her," she screamed.

I asked her to please take off the diaper. She opened the left side of the diaper and closed it within seconds, which led me to believe there was something illegal on the baby.

"Paula," I said, "we need you to remove the entire diaper." I told her I would post a female officer with her due to privacy concerns, and Paula reluctantly agreed.

The female officer saw Paula remove the diaper, and it was apparent there was a bowel movement present. However, Paula quickly closed the diaper again, obviously scared and frightened.

The female officer then insisted that Paula totally remove the diaper.

Paula exhaled, realizing the jig was up. She opened the diaper, and the female officer saw a pink zipper pouch that had been contained in the soiled diaper. The officer called me into the room, and Paula began screaming that the pouch contained only rings and not drugs.

The female officer opened the pouch and did discover eighteen rings. Along with seven grams of methamphetamine.

Paula became hysterical at this point, screaming, "I didn't know there were drugs in that pouch!"

The female officer became enraged and began lecturing Paula, while drowning out her screams. "How dare you hide drugs on this child. You are the worst excuse for a human being I have ever seen," the female officer screamed. "What were you thinking? This baby is an angel, and you hide your fucking drugs down her diaper?"

The female officer was getting more intense, while staring Paula down. The officer was body posturing Paula to fall onto the bed, while the intensity of her lecturing grew even stronger.

It reached a point where I subtly pulled the officer off Paula and told her to leave the room. I wasn't sure what the female officer was planning on doing next, but I knew it was not good. I had never seen the officer this upset before.

I handcuffed Paula and told her she was under arrest. I recall saying, "You are lucky I took that female officer off your ass."

Paula became hysterical, claiming she had no clue there were drugs in the zipper pouch. Before I handcuffed Paula, she attempted to grab the naked baby and use her as a shield between us. I was able to safely place the baby on the bed and get Paula secured.

Paula was screaming, "Come on, Langan. Let me go and I can set you up with a ten-pound deal!"

Ever the drug dealer, Paula was still wanting to barter her charges, even though she had just hidden methamphetamine down the diaper of her severely disabled granddaughter. I refused to consider her offer.

Both Paula and Chico did substantial federal prison time.

And I will always love my grandchildren more than life itself.

11

DON'T PICK ON ME

Have you ever noticed how firefighters love to advertise on their personal cars that they are, in fact, firefighters? Most have the national firefighter decal on the back window of their cars and trucks. Or bumper stickers that say slogans like "I Love My Firefighter" or "Support Your Local Firefighter."

The reason for this is obvious to most cops. Everybody loves firefighters!

After all, what's not to like about them? Whenever a citizen has an encounter with the fire department, they know that help is on the way. And, afterward, they don't get locked up in a dirty, stinky jail cell like they do when they deal with cops.

Firefighters pull old ladies from burning houses, grab cats out of trees, and save people who are dying from heart attacks.

Cops write tickets for running red lights, chastise partygoers to keep the noise down, and zap perps with tasers.

Most cops do not advertise what they do for a living. I have never seen a bumper sticker that says, "I Love Being a Cop" or "Police Officer on Board."

To do so creates the risk of the cop's personal car being keyed, pissed on, or spray-painted with the word *PIG*.

Women go crazy for firemen. The stereotype of a male firefighter is young, virile, and buffed out. After all, look at all the downtime they have in the firehouses. What else is there to do but workout?

Cops, on the other hand, are on the street 24/7, racing from call to call to call, with hardly enough time to get a decent meal. The reputation of loving donuts is not always accurate, but I will admit most cops are not perceived as being lady killers, at least not as much as our brother firefighters.

The rivalry between police officers and firefighters goes back generations. Both swear an oath to protect the public but do so in distinctly different ways.

I admit, I am biased toward police officers, who will risk their lives by running into a burning building to save lives, even though this is the job of the fire department. But I am also keenly aware that the rivalry and, at times, bad feelings between police officers and firefighters only goes so far.

When there's a job to be done, both will do it with total professionalism. This is especially true when one needs the help of the other.

OFFICER DOWN

A few years back, an Omaha Police officer was shot in the stomach during a traffic stop. He was lying in the street, bleeding out, and being helped by a civilian who was close by. The officer was able to call for help.

The frantic call came out over the police radio. Words that police officers never want to hear on the radio: "Help an officer. Officer down."

Police cars were racing from all directions. Within two minutes of the officer's call for help, rescuers with Omaha Fire Engine 21 were at the scene. But already the officer was struggling for life. Rescuers began working to control his bleeding and keep his airway open. Soon he was in the back of an ambulance and on the way to the hospital.

The firefighters and paramedics saved his life by stopping the bleeding and rushing him to a trauma center. After four hours of surgery and twenty units of blood, twice a person's blood volume, the officer survived.

Countless times across our country, paramedics and firefighters have saved the lives of police officers who have been shot, stabbed, or struck by a fleeing vehicle.

Countless times police officers have been there to save the day for firefighters pinned down by a sniper, or those involved in the fight of their lives with a suspect under the influence of PCP.

Police officers are always going to kid firefighters about being "hose jockeys" and being underworked. Firefighters will always chide cops about eating too many donuts.

I end with this thought.

It is okay for cops to pick on hose jockeys and vice versa. That is because we're in the arena together, facing dangers that most others cannot handle or comprehend.

But if you are not in the circle, I suggest you be careful picking on my fellow brothers and sisters who fight fires and saves lives every day. I have a huge respect for firefighters, even though, as a former cop, it is tough to admit at times.

Remember the old saying, "I can talk trash about my family all day, but if you say the wrong thing about my family, you may end up with a black eye."

12

HUMMEL PARK: ENTER AT YOUR OWN RISK

Rumor had it that a low, mournful moaning could be heard coming from an old rickety bridge late at night in Hummel Park.

Hummel Park is an enormous city park that sits high atop a bluff overlooking the Missouri River just north of Omaha.

In 1977 my high school graduation class from Roncalli High School held an all-night retreat at a beautiful center owned by Creighton University built at the top of Hummel Park. Around 1:00 a.m. a bunch of us snuck out and walked side-by-side down the pitch-black roads that wound through the heavily wooded park.

The wind was from the south when suddenly we heard the low-pitched moan, rising to a high-pitched scream coming from the area of what came to be known as Screaming Angel Bridge. I about pissed my pants, and we high-tailed it back to the sanctity and safety of the retreat center.

In 1985 I was called back to the park in my duties as a detective with the organized crime/intelligence unit of the Omaha Police Department for activity equally as spooky. Only now I was a cop carrying a gun.

Besides working outlaw motorcycle gangs, gambling, and prostitution cases, the unit was a catch-all squad. If a tip came in about an obscure situation that didn't fall under the normal types of crimes, we would get the case.

Such a tip was received in September that year when a caller reported satanic cult activity taking place late at night in the park. Normally, Satan worshipping is not considered to be criminal activity. Even though it borders on the bizarre, police normally will not become involved in monitoring satanic activity or other religious ceremonies, unless extenuating circumstances exist.

However, the caller added a spicy tidbit to the initial information. According to the tipster, the satanic worshippers were sacrificing cats during the midnight ceremony in the dark, secluded pavilion of the infamous venue. Killing animals during such a ceremony would be considered animal cruelty, which is a crime. A police response was both necessary and proper yet posed logistical nightmares.

The park itself is a 200-acre parcel with narrow, poorly paved roads that wind endlessly from one secluded area to another. It is one of the few parks in Omaha that is heavily wooded, with hiking trails and a Missouri River overlook. The park is home to Devil's Slide, a dirt cliff that had been rumored to be the suicide site of motorcyclists and despondent persons alike.

In my day, most Omaha Police officers did not conduct routine patrols in Hummel Park for the simple reason that if they found someone engaged in criminal activity (which would be a good bet), it would take forever for the backup units to find the officer who needed help. Roads are not marked, and there are plenty of twists and turns, which made it tough to locate an officer who might be getting his butt kicked in the park.

Hummel Park has been the site of violent homicides over the years, as well as sexual assaults, stolen car drop-offs, and general debauchery. For over forty years I have cruised Hummel Park. It is not uncommon to find empty beer cans, various articles of female clothing, and used condoms littering the parking lots throughout the park.

Entrance to Hummel Park.

THE LEGENDS LIVE ON

More than being famous for criminal and sexual activity, Hummel Park is the site for such urban legends as these, in addition to the Screaming Angel Bridge:

- The infamous hermit, whom I first heard about in high school in the late 1970s, lived in a cave in the side of a ravine and only came out at night to peer in car windows at teens swapping spit. Unfortunately, I was not one of those teens.

- Native American burial grounds are rumored to be part of Hummel Park. At certain times scofflaws like me who violated the 11:00 p.m. park curfew heard the repetitive pounding of drums and wolves howling in the far distance. It was scarier than crap, but great fun at the same time.

- Of course, the most famous legend of Hummel Park, promoted for years by generations of North Omahans, involved the albino farm. The story goes like this: A group of albinos hides during the day and at night come out from a secluded farm to tend to their crops and to troll through the forests of Hummel Park. Now I realize forty years later how harmful these rumors were to the several albino kids I knew living in the North Omaha area.

So when the tip of the cat-killing satanic worshippers was phoned in, I was quick to volunteer for the strange assignment. After all, I was a North Omaha kid who knew Hummel Park like the back of my hand. I was perfect for this assignment.

My partner and I drove into the park around 10:30 on the cold, crisp Saturday night. We decided to park our undercover car in a lower lot to the west of the pavilion where the suspected satanic activity took place. I was dressed in all black from head to toe, complete with my utility belt that held my holster with a .38 pistol, extra ammunition, and handcuffs.

It was so dark I had a hard time finding my utility case that held my binoculars and, most importantly, the night vision scope that would allow us to watch through the darkness for what was going to transpire in the pavilion at midnight.

Compared to current equipment, the night vision scope we had in 1985 was antiquated, but as far as we knew at the time it was the most advanced equipment available for an assignment like this. I would be able to look through the scope and see a green screen with silhouettes of human beings in the pavilion. I worried that I might not be able to distinguish cats being tortured and sacrificed, but I figured the felines' high-pitched shrieks would travel through the park just as the Screaming Angel's moans and screams had done for many years.

Next, my partner and I climbed the 180-plus stone steps leading from the lower bowl of Hummel Park to the pavilion at the park's highest point. Known at the Morphing Steps of Hummel Park, folklore has it that there are always more steps to count when you climb to the top than when you descend to the bottom.

Climbing the Morphing Steps in 2020.

We dared not use flashlights for fear of being detected by early-arriving Satan worshippers. Luckily, a clear sky offered moonlight that illuminated the steps as we slowly climbed step-by-step, trying not to stumble in the process. Even though my partner and I were together, and armed with guns, I vividly remember being scared as we ascended higher to the top of the park.

Was the Hummel Park hermit lurking near us, undiscernible in the darkness? Were Native American spirits walking next to us, daring me to step off the path onto their sacred grounds? The thoughts crossed my mind.

Finally, we reached the top and saw the outline of the pavilion in the distance. It was eerily quiet, with no cars in the parking lot. We decided to crawl close to a tree line about a hundred feet to the south of the pavilion, near the Morphing Steps. The tree line offered us concealment in the dark as well as an unobstructed view of the south end of the stone pavilion. I felt safe that anyone parking and walking to the pavilion would not be able to see us lying along the trees in the darkness.

The pavilion in Hummel Park, site of the satanic rituals.

Boy, I was glad my partner was next to me.

"Listen," I said, "did you hear the cracking sounds in the woods? Is someone walking up behind us?"

"Shut up or you're going to get us killed," my partner said, showing me that he knew nothing of, nor was he impressed with, the legends of Hummel Park.

Back in the 1980s the Omaha Police Department radio system was well known among cops to have dead spots in certain parts of the city. These were areas of town where the radio towers, placed throughout the city, did not provide coverage for officers who needed to transmit important information. Hummel Park was such an area, which was the primary reason why officers avoided doing routine patrols by themselves.

We realized our portable radio would not work, and even if it did, 1985 was years away from earpieces that connected to the radio. With the stiff south wind, we knew our portable radio would certainly be heard in the distance by the worshippers, even if we had the volume down low. We simply could not risk using the radio.

Finally, we were set up in our surveillance spot. We laid on our bellies for fear of the moonlight exposing our bodies if we stood. The night vision scope was working well. It was getting cold, but we had several layers of clothes on to keep us warm.

Now we waited.

OF ROBES AND PENTACLES

Minutes passed and the temperatures dropped. It was windy and chilly, and I began wondering why the hell I volunteered for this assignment. As time passed, we doubted that anyone was going to show up. It was getting late and cold, and we were growing impatient.

Shortly before midnight, headlights approached the small parking lot to the east of the pavilion. My heart starting racing as I realized that the tip phoned into the organized crime/intelligence unit might have some merit to it.

Several cars parked and shut off their headlights. Nobody got out, but we could see more than one silhouette in each car through the night vision scope.

A couple of minutes later three or four more cars pulled up, and people started getting out. It was a curious sight to take in. They all wore black robes with hoods covering their heads. I will never forget the images through the scope of the dozen or so worshippers walking through the park wearing their intimidating garb. They said little as they entered the pavilion.

Immediately, candles were lit on a picnic table in the middle of the open-air stone pavilion. We watched as the worshippers formed a circle and began a low, mournful chant that went on for over an hour. They seemed to change the incantation every ten to fifteen minutes, moving in circles around the table.

Their concentration seemed to be fixated on the picnic table. However, since they were huddled together wearing thick black robes, we could not make out what they were doing. Was a cat being gutted right in front of us? We thought not, since we could not hear any cat-like screams piercing the night air.

I remember thinking this was an unbelievable sight. Here we were, a hundred feet away from a group of Satan worshippers who had no idea they were being watched through a night vision scope by two freezing cold Omaha Police officers.

Certainly, we could jump up and charge into the pavilion yelling, "Police, you are all under arrest for violation of park curfew." After all, the park closed to the public at 11:00 p.m.

To do that would have been suicide. We were outnumbered twelve to two, in a secluded park where our police radios did not work. We felt semi-safe where we were and had no intention of moving.

We also realized that we had not planned this operation well from the very beginning. What if we did see or hear a cat being sacrificed by the satanic cult? What was the plan? Where was our backup?

Actually, we had no plan. We had no backup. We were on our own and in no position to arrest anybody or even to call for help. Cell phones and GPS were a long way from being available.

I was scared we would end up being sacrificed if we were stupid enough to divulge our location. Hopefully, a cat was not involved in this weird ritual because, if it was, we were not going to rescue it.

The bladders of satanic worshippers are no different than other humans. Several times one of them walked outside the pavilion to relieve themselves. The guys had it easier than the women given the ankle-long robes they were wearing.

One of the more modest participants walked a bit farther away from the pavilion, eventually pissing about twenty feet from our surveillance position. We held our breath as we heard his stream hitting the ground near us, and the smell of urine filled the air. This guy had no clue how close he was to us. It was so dark he would have peed on top of us if he walked a little more to the south.

After an hour, the candles were blown out and the robes came off. The worshippers walked to their cars and left the park. Finally, my partner and I could stand up, stretch, and pee.

A few minutes later we carefully walked into the pavilion to check for any evidence of cat worshipping left behind. Luckily, we determined no cats had been sacrificed, at least not on this night. We found that a pentacle had been carved into the picnic table. The pentacle is a star-like symbol enclosed in a circle and is often used to represent Satanism.

We finally left the park after descending the Morphing Steps. I was relieved to lock the doors to our car as I drove down the dark, winding roads. I had felt vulnerable for too long in the legendary Omaha location known as Hummel Park.

Decades later, while writing this story, I visited Hummel Park and traversed the Morphing Steps—during the day. My plan was to count the same number of steps climbing down as when I climbed up. On the way down I counted 186 steps. I then slowly climbed back up, intently counting one step after another so as not to throw off my tally. The final count on the way to the top was 188 steps.

I laughed to myself while noticing my shortness of breath as a fifty-seven-year-old compared to my youthful ascent in 1985.

The legend of the Morphing Steps lives on.

Shortly after I began my second career as the top cop for the Nebraska Humane Society, I worked with the Omaha Police Department on arresting a person for killing a cat and dissecting the animal's organs. We found various body parts in plastic containers in the freezer of his house.

The investigation determined the guy was a practicing pagan. Historic pagan rituals include animal sacrifices and the use of both blood and meat from the animal in a ceremony known as the Viking Blood Sacrifice. The investigation took me back twenty-one years earlier to the darkness of Hummel Park.

13

LIAR, LIAR, PANTS ON FIRE

People lie to cops all the time.

They lie about their name.

They lie about their birthday, where they live, who they are with, why they are with the person they claim not to know, and just about anything else they can think to lie about.

I told suspects, "You're telling me so many lies that you can't remember the first few lies you told me. So why don't you just tell me the truth?"

Many times, they did.

My favorite lies were the ones that were so blatantly false they caused me and the other cops to laugh out loud.

Us: "I'm arresting you based on the cocaine found in your pants!"

Bad Guy: "Hold on, man, these are not my pants!"

Us: "But you're wearing the pants, sir."

Bad Guy: "I know, I know, but listen up. I found these pants and just put them on."

Or even better.

Us: "You're under arrest for the ounce of crack the doctor just pulled out of your ass."

Bad Guy: "Man, that's not my dope."

Us: "If it's not your dope, how did it end up in your ass?"

Bad Guy: "Man, you motherfuckers planted it there!"

Us: "Let me get this straight. You're telling me I shoved a golf-ball–sized baggie of crack up your ass without you knowing about it?"

And the lies kept coming.

Judge Walter Cropper was a stalwart jurist for the Douglas County Court in Omaha, Nebraska.

He was known for a baritone voice that bellowed throughout the courtroom, as well as his somewhat sarcastic quips and stories he would tell certain defendants that stood in front of him.

Many times, he leaned over the bench and glared into the eyes of cocky guys who were not taking the court proceedings seriously.

"Young man," he would say, "if you want to stay out of my courtroom, I suggest you do the following. Keep your hands in your pockets, your mouth shut, and your zipper zipped, and you'll never see me again in your entire life."

One time Judge Cropper was hearing a case of a young man charged with possessing a gun. It was found under the front seat of the car he was driving, but he was maintaining it was not his gun.

"Let me tell you a little story," Judge Cropper said to the defendant.

Once there was a newspaper boy delivering papers in the neighborhood. He walks up to a house that has a fenced-in front yard. There's an old man rocking in his chair on the porch, with an old junkyard dog lying at his feet.

"Hey, old man," the kid yells, "does your dog bite?"

"Nope," the old man mutters.

So the newspaper boy opens the gate and begins walking up the sidewalk to the front porch so he can hand the paper to the old man.

The dog springs up and charges at the kid, barking and growling while chasing him back toward the sidewalk. The dog nips the kid in the butt just before he slams the gate shut.

The kid is now shaking and notices the tear in his jeans.

"Hey, old man," he angrily yells, "I thought you said your dog didn't bite!"

The old man replies, "Not my dog."

Bang.

Judge Cropper slammed his gavel and exclaimed, "Guilty."

The kid did thirty days in the gray-bar hotel.

14

LIKE A THOUSAND RAILROAD TRAINS

During my career as a police officer I always found it fascinating how people gravitated into drug use and drug dealing, and how they dealt with the resultant descent into the black hole.

I never considered it appropriate or ethical to simply arrest someone and forget about them, especially if the suspect had an interesting story to tell.

How did they fall into this lifestyle? Was it generational? Did the young girl learn to inject herself with methamphetamine from her parents? Did her father trick her out in order to satisfy his cravings? What was the defining moment in their lives that caused them to take the wrong turn when approaching that proverbial fork in the road?

These were but some of the questions I asked many people I arrested, and I found the answers enlightening.

In 2016 I was talking to a group of citizens about my book, *Busting Bad Guys*. I watched an older guy in the crowd react to many of my stories by either shaking his head or laughing to himself. He had a biker look to him, with a salt-and-pepper goatee and longer hair. He was a bigger guy with an intimidating stare, which he flashed at me as my talk progressed.

I could not make out if he was being sarcastic with his reactions, or if I was hitting a nerve with him. Either way, I remember thinking this was a guy I needed to keep an eye on.

After I was done talking to the group, he approached me with a big smile and extended a handshake. Once he told me his name, I remembered him well.

In his previous life Roger was one of the most well-known drug dealers in Omaha. My crew and other law enforcement agencies had targeted him for years. Finally, we arrested him toward the end of my career, and Roger was sentenced to ten years in federal prison.

I have written this before, but it bears repeating. It is amazing how many bad guys I have arrested that reappear in my life years later. Most, like Roger, make a point of initiating the contact. And, like Roger, most thank me and the officers involved for saving their lives. It is truly inspiring stuff.

ROGER'S DRUG STORY

Roger agreed to sit down and tell me his life story. His deep, gravelly voice confirmed to me a hard life of drinking, smoking, and drugs.

I wrongly assumed that Roger had been raised in a household fraught with drug use and criminal activity, as is the case of so many others I have arrested.

Instead, Roger grew up in a middle-class Protestant family in the picturesque Dundee neighborhood of midtown Omaha. Dundee is one of the older neighborhoods in Omaha, established in 1880, and many of the houses are close to a hundred years old. Most homes on Roger's block were stately two-story structures with manicured yards and wood-framed detached garages. Within blocks were vibrant shops, stores, and bars that provided a constant energy to the Dundee neighborhood.

His parents were hard workers, and Roger and his brother did not go without the necessities that teenage boys needed in the 1970s. Though not from a wealthy family, Roger lacked for nothing.

Church was a big part of their lives. He told me, "My family was very church oriented. I never really took to that, but it was a big part of my upbringing."

But like many children of the 1960s and 1970s, Roger fell into the wrong crowd and began experimenting with alcohol and marijuana around age fifteen.

"I started out by sneaking a few beers out of the fridge and smoking cigarettes."

This comment rang so true to me. In so many interviews with career criminals I conducted over the years, many seemed to tell a similar story—starting out as preteens smoking cigarettes, then moving on to smoking marijuana. This was followed by selling marijuana, and then methamphetamine and cocaine entered the picture.

Then, at a certain pivotal point in their life, they met me and went to prison.

Roger's story was eerily similar. He was fifteen when he started smoking marijuana.

"On the weekends we'd get out and find somebody to buy beer for us and we *always* knew who was selling weed," he said.

As our interview began, Roger wanted to tell me about a devastating moment in his early life, one that he blames for catapulting him into the dark world of drug use and drug dealing. I could immediately tell this was painful for him, so I was patient in letting him tell the story.

"After I graduated high school," he said, "my parents finally decided my brother and I were old enough to where they could leave us alone for a period of time. They thought we were mature enough. Sadly, I wasn't."

His parents left for a two-week trip to the East Coast, with stern rules in place for Roger and his older brother.

"Oh my God, for two months before they left, every sentence ended with 'and no parties while we are gone.' So the first thing I did after they left was—I had a party."

A friend of Roger's brother was commissioned to buy a sixteen-gallon keg of beer "and a couple of cases of tall boys, just in case."

Roger's parents left on a Wednesday, and the party was on Friday.

"It was a helluva party. We burned through the keg and the tall boys, and it was getting to be 12:30." Roger knew the bars closed at 1:00 a.m., so he devised a plan to keep the party going.

"I started begging my brother's best friend to get us more beer. He'd hung out with us most of the night, and he was pretty drunk, as we all were. He really didn't want to go, but I talked him into going, gave him some money, and sent him on his way."

Roger's life changed forever in the next few minutes. After his inebriated buddy bought three cases of beer, strapped them to the back of his motorcycle and headed back to the party, he was killed when he struck a pickup truck near Saddle Creek Road and Leavenworth Street.

"The worst thing in the world I ever had to do was wake my brother up and tell him I basically killed his friend. And the look on my brother's face ... I'll never forget that. It was crushing."

Roger was sixteen years old.

"He was dead and buried before my parents got home from their trip. My God, the pain and anguish and guilt I felt was just overwhelming," he said.

A FATAL ACCIDENT, A LIFE OF GRIEF

From that point on, Roger's life took a turn for the worse and would do so for the next twenty-five years.

After his friend died, "I pretty much started drinking and smoking pot the whole time."

Roger's dad, a former marine drill sergeant, had some encouraging words for his son. "He flat-out told me, 'It's not your fault. This friend was one of those guys who would fly through intersections on his motorcycle.' And from then on, nobody wanted to bring it up to me. In those days there was no therapy like there is now, so everybody just tucked it away, including my brother and I."

Roger tried college for a while, but soon dropped out due to ever-worsening depression fueled by increased drug use. He said, "I did nothing but drink and smoke pot that first year, and I got kicked out."

At age nineteen he was introduced to methamphetamine inside the bathroom of a midtown Omaha dive bar. This would change his life forever.

"Boy howdy, that was a whole new experience, up for hours and hours. I couldn't get enough of the stuff. That was my intro-duction to crank." On the street, methamphetamine has been known as crank for years.

He also fell in love with cocaine at the same time but noticed a distinct difference between the two stimulant drugs.

"Oh, cocaine didn't last near as long. Cocaine, you could snort a line and be ready to snort another one in an hour. You can go through a lot of cocaine. You can do a line of metham-phetamine and go for twenty-four hours easily."

According to Roger, back in the late 1970s methamphet-amine was known as the poor man's cocaine.

Once Roger started talking of his early days of using meth and cocaine, his stories became more colorful and harder to believe, even for a seasoned cop like myself.

"We had a friend in medical school in Omaha, and he had access to a vat of 90 percent pure liquid cocaine from the ENT department. He was coming home every night with syringes full of cocaine. That was some tremendous stuff."

Roger enrolled at another Omaha university, and his illicit tastes now included cocaine, methamphetamine, LSD, hallu-cinogenic mushrooms, and mescaline. His fraternity brothers were mainly pot smokers, "but nobody had the tastes I did."

Soon Roger quit college for good, and he began tending bar at various known drug bars around the midtown area.

"Is this how you began selling drugs?" I asked.

"Yeah, because somebody's turning you onto a little bit every night. And then you have people asking you all the time, 'Hey can you find any?' And then it doesn't take long to figure out that if I buy an eight-ball, I can sell a couple of grams and do mine for free."

A smart drug dealer can make easy money. Roger was paying $200 for an eight-ball of methamphetamine in the early 1980s. Eight-ball is slang for one-eighth ounce of meth, or 3.5 grams. Roger learned he could sell two of the grams for $100 each and recoup his initial investment. That left 1.5 grams for his personal use, which he basically used for free. He could repeat this cycle over and over and never be in debt to his dealer.

GETTING HIGH ON THE JET PLANES

Soon Roger left the bartending world for a great job working for a large airline at Omaha's Eppley Airfield. Lucky for him there were no drug tests involved, so he was able to work the graveyard shift on the secured side of the airport all by himself for the most part.

His job during the winter was to keep the airplanes warm so the lines wouldn't freeze.

"I'd have to drag these big four-wheeled trailers with huge generators and plug them into the belly of the plane to keep things warm. We had three planes and only two heaters, so they taught me how to fire up a DC-9 jet to keep it warm. Plus, since I was by myself, I was smoking pot all night enjoying looking at all the blue lights on the runway."

I said, "So let me get this straight. You're working for a major airline in the graveyard shift, an important job on the secured side of the airport, and you're servicing planes and smoking pot while you are working?"

With a smirk Roger replied, "Oh, it gets worse. I was still pretty famous with the bar scene, and my buddies would call me and say, 'Hey, is the coast clear down there? We have a rolling party.'"

"Bring it down," Roger would tell them.

Roger explained that after 2:00 a.m. the strip clubs closed in neighboring Council Bluffs, Iowa, so his buddies would bring a contingent of dancers down to Eppley Airfield where they would meet up with Roger.

Keep in mind, this was at least twenty years before the terror attacks of September 11, 2001, and security at the time was much looser.

"Party on the plane," Roger gleefully told me. "Tray tables down and cutting lines of cocaine on them."

Roger indicated there were all types of debauchery taking place on the planes, and at a certain point he knew he needed to get his friends off the plane since the first flight time was approaching.

"Oh my God, what a nightmare! There were so many times I did not think I was going to get those guys out of there and get everything cleaned up."

I had to ask Roger, "So when passengers got on the plane that morning and dropped their tray tables, they had no idea there was probably cocaine residue present?"

"I'd hate to think what the customers might have found on those tray tables and the seat cushions," he said.

WE DELIVER

Soon Roger found himself working in downtown Omaha at the main branch of the United States Post Office.

The stories just kept coming.

He was working the afternoon shift, as this schedule fit perfectly with his ever-growing lifestyle of methamphetamine and cocaine use.

"There were no shortages of drugs at the post office. I have never worked in a more drug-infested, alcohol-infested place in my life. Especially the old timers. It was just amazing how many of them had a jug of Jack Daniels in their lockers. The first thing they did was punch in, buy Coca-Cola, and make themselves a nice little all-day toddy," he said.

"Those of us who did meth never had to leave the building [post office] because we knew where to go and what bathrooms to meet up in."

After work, he and his coworkers continued their hard-driving lifestyle by closing the nearby Iowa bars at 2:00 a.m.

Roger was fired six years into his postal career for punching out a supervisor. Roger had run out the wrong emergency exit during a fire drill in the building, and as a result the supervisor called him out in front of other employees at a safety meeting the following week.

Roger admitted he was being a bit sarcastic to the supervisor in front of the other employees, which did not help his cause with the boss.

"He grabbed my arm, causing me to jerk away and then I dropped him," Roger said. "And I admit I had a nose full of crank or else I would have never done that."

Roger went back to his workstation, knowing he had not heard the end of the situation. Sure enough, several hours later, five United States Postal Inspectors approached him and escorted him out of the building.

Roger cockily told them, "I'll give you ten minutes to get more guys," but then quickly laughed at them and said, "I'm just kidding."

Roger left the building and never found gainful employment again. By this point in Roger's life he had been using drugs for twenty years. Marijuana, cocaine, methamphetamine, LSD, and mescaline had taken over his life.

HELLO, ETERNAL DARKNESS

As if things could not get any worse, they did. He met a woman who introduced him to the eternal darkness known as the hypodermic needle.

"What caused you to start banging?" I asked Roger. Banging is the street term for injecting drugs. Why? Because the effects hit quickly, within seconds. The downside, of course, other than drug use itself, is the risk for disease caused by needle use (hepatitis and AIDS) and addiction, overdose, and death.

"A girl," he admitted. "She wooed me by telling me, 'Hey, let me turn you onto this, it's really great.'"

Roger had been using drugs for many years and had seen plenty of addicts using a hypodermic needle. But it never appealed to him until the alluring female convinced him to enjoy the new effects, along with the fringe benefits she included in her proposition.

I told him to tell me about the first time he banged meth with a needle.

"John Prine wrote a song called 'Sam Stone' about a Vietnam vet coming home from war with a drug habit. The song says the gold rolled through his veins like a thousand railroad trains," Roger said. "I'll tell you what, Mark, it don't get any closer than that. It's like starting the motor on a big, beefy V8 and it just comes to life. And it's instantaneous, it's unbelievable."

For twenty years prior to meeting the needle, Roger was a functioning alcoholic and drug addict. But once that needle hit his vein, everything changed.

"I always worked, always maintained a normal façade of a lifestyle, and still showed up for family functions and dinners. But, boy, once I started banging, I didn't have much to do with family or friends. When the needles started, the wheels started coming off."

Today, Roger is a recovering drug addict. After leaving federal prison he never used or sold drugs again. At least that's what he tells me. And I believe him.

During my interviews with him I saw through his hardened exterior and noticed a sensitive, motivated man who has goals in life and a plan to reach them.

He is now a supervisor with a prosperous and privately owned company in Omaha. He has a crew of employees that report to him.

Roger told me there is rampant drug use where he works. The temptation is always there.

"Let me tell you about meth," Roger said. "After the first few times you try, you will never get that same high again. But you'll spend the rest of your life chasing it."

15

THE OTHER WOMAN REVISITED

magine a woman hidden in a basement-level secret room right under the nose of a drug dealer's unsuspecting wife.

One of the stories most talked about in my first book is titled "The Other Woman."

It deals with the Omaha drug dealer who, besides possessing lots of drugs and weapons, was found to be hiding a woman in his basement unbeknownst to his wife. In my numerous book appearances, many women have relayed to me how, after reading that story, they've gone over every square inch of their family abodes, not because they didn't trust their husbands, but … just for peace of mind.

In 2016 I was signing books at a busy event when I noticed an attractive woman walking toward my table with a confident gait and a glint in her eye. Her youthful appearance belied the fact she was in her middle forties. She was dressed in a red pull-over sweater and blue jeans. She was a bit short and had a nice shape to her. Her long straight brown hair had blonde streaks, and the smile on her face told me she had something really exciting to tell me.

Problem was, I had no clue who she was.

"Mark, you probably don't remember me, but you actually write about me in your book," she said.

I admitted to her that I was stumped, and she was quick to solve the mystery.

"I'm the ex-wife of the guy who hid the girl in my basement," she exclaimed, almost laughing with joy while she dropped the news on me.

It was immediately obvious that this lady had nothing to be embarrassed about, and she was overjoyed at accidentally running into me. She was giddy to buy a book, and I penned a special inscription to her saying this: "Life comes full circle in strange and glorious ways!"

We laughed when I brought up how fifteen years earlier we never could have imagined we would be excited to see each other again.

I was even more amazed when she agreed to sit with me to discuss the ups and downs of her life, starting with why she married this guy, seeing him gradually gravitate into a dark hole, and finally trying to put her life back together after we tore her house—and life—apart on that cold March day in 2001.

Most importantly, she was willing to answer the burning questions that many of my readers asked: How did she feel when she discovered her husband was hiding his tweaked-out methamphetamine-addicted girlfriend in the house she shared with him and their three small daughters? And how could she not have known this woman was being hidden in her own house while at the same time not suspecting her husband was selling drugs?

Before I tell you those answers, let me summarize the original story.

THE OTHER WOMAN

Methamphetamine, semi-automatic rifles, and large amounts of cash.

During my police career, I was surprised if we did not find these together during the hundreds of search warrants I did.

Elaborate surveillance systems, hidden outdoor microphones, and bulletproof vests.

It certainly was not out of the ordinary for the methamphetamine dealer to do whatever he thought necessary to protect his operation.

A hidden room in the basement, used to hide another woman while the dealer's wife was at home?

Now that was a first, even for a guy like me who thought he had seen it all.

We had been after this guy for years, knowing he was selling large amounts of methamphetamine out of his north central Omaha home. Finally, an informant gave us the information we needed to obtain a search warrant.

The informant told us this guy would start selling meth after his wife left for work in the morning. When she returned home in the afternoon, the shop was closed.

[SWAT units helped in the raid because this dealer had high-powered weapons in the house and outside surveillance cameras.]

The suspect and a "customer" were found cowering in the basement next to two surveillance monitors showing different views of the outside of the house ...

We found meth, money, guns, and bulletproof vests. He hung his head in defeat, knowing life as he knew it was over.

After several minutes I noticed one of my guys standing near a dresser along the wood paneling of the basement. He was intently looking at the wall, so I asked what was piquing his interest.

Without answering he moved the dresser back, grabbed a piece of the paneling, and slowly opened a hidden door. None of us had noticed this, as the cracks in the door blended into the wood paneling.

I was shocked to see a woman huddled in a fetal position in the corner of a small room. On the floor was a dirty mattress next to a couple of glass jars filled with urine.

The lady was in her thirties, and she looked like hell. Her hair was dirty and unkempt. The clothes she wore appeared not to have been washed recently. We located methamphetamine paraphernalia in the hidden room, which went a long way to explain her appearance.

It turns out the dealer was allowing this girl to live in this hidden room, right under his wife's nose. When the wife was home, or drug customers came to buy methamphetamine, the girl was secreted away. When the wife was gone, she was allowed out of the room to do her thing, whatever that was. She peed in the glass jars and smoked methamphetamine to while away the hours.

After we had been in the house for a while, the guy's wife came home. She claimed she was shocked to see us there, denying any knowledge of her husband's illegal activity.

I walked with her to the basement, allowing her to see her handcuffed husband.

Upon seeing the meth-head female, the wife exclaimed, "Who the hell is this?"

THE REST OF THE STORY

The wife, Staci, told me the rest of the story.

"I don't care what happens to you. I hope you go kill yourself and die in the street!" were the first words Staci screamed at her husband, after he bonded out from jail three days after the drug raid.

Staci was pissed and let her husband know it. After posting bond, he returned to their Omaha Benson-area house, a quiet midtown neighborhood.

"It was awful," Staci said. "It was the first time I had a chance to see him and confront him and I think every emotion that could possibly come out, came out. I punched him until my hands were bruised. I had chest pains, and I had no voice. I was so angry!

"I yelled at him, 'How could you do this to me? How could you do this to these kids? They could have been hurt!'"

I asked Staci how her husband responded.

"Oh, he shut down. He cried, 'I'm sorry.' He's blocking my punches and crying, 'I'm so sorry.'"

Staci first met her husband when she was eighteen and he was twenty-one. They were both at Peony Park in Omaha, a great place in the summer for teens to congregate, socialize, and dance the night away during the Sprite Night music events.

Her husband was a tall good-looking guy with dark brown hair and a smile that melted her heart.

Staci told me that she felt an immediate attraction, and the relationship grew quickly.

Soon they married, much to the chagrin of her father, a military man who was protective of his daughter.

"You know, my dad was right. He told me, 'You don't have to go through with this,' before he walked me down the aisle."

Staci said even though she saw no open drug use or dealing by her husband early in their relationship, there were signs that now, as an adult, she wished she would have recognized.

"There were things that bothered me, and I questioned, but in the mind of a teenager, I didn't think much of," she said. "When he worked, he wasn't gainfully employed, so he said he worked part-time construction."

As Staci's relationship ebbed and flowed with her husband over the years, she grew to realize that many of his drug-dealing associates also used the façade of "working construction" as justification for their purpose in life.

Staci's comments rang true with me. Many drug dealers I arrested over the years claimed to work part-time for construction crews, though they seldom did.

Another popular occupation among drug dealers was selling cars. It seemed like car dealerships would hire just about anybody, and it was common for these employees to bounce from one car lot to another. The drug-dealing network among car sellers was amazing.

Years ago, I bought a new car, and just as I signed the paperwork, the young salesperson told me how I had arrested her several years earlier for selling drugs. To this day, I hate buying cars.

Staci admitted to recreational drug use after she met her husband. She had never tried drugs before the relationship. She said, "I did not experiment with drugs until I met him. But as far as methamphetamine, no!"

Looking back on their relationship, she said, "He never really seemed to have goals in life, never seemed to want to get ahead in life, and when I met his family, I think that was a telling sign that maybe these individuals probably were not goal oriented."

In fact, her husband's parents were drug dealers themselves, both serving prison sentences during Staci's marriage.

In the beginning Staci had misgivings about her future in-laws. "I just remember thinking they were kind of trashy."

Staci's father had a low impression of her future in-laws prior to her wedding too. "My father-in-law at the time had to have permission to attend our wedding because he was incarcerated. I remember my dad was just disgusted by the whole situation. My dad told me he tried to make small talk with my father-in-law, but he later told me, 'You know, that asshole didn't even shake my hand.'"

Early in her marriage Staci sat in the courtroom as wiretap conversations were played of her in-laws negotiating large-scale drug deals with some of the most dangerous criminals on the streets of Omaha.

"I remember listening to the wiretaps about guns, silencers, and I could hear my mother-in-law and father-in-law on tape making transactions. It was interesting to see some of the people that were in court. I think the drug culture itself, it's interesting in some way, I suppose," she told me.

NO OBVIOUS SIGNS OF DRUG USE

Staci and her husband were married for ten years before the police raided her house and changed their lives forever. During

that time, she was gainfully employed as a healthcare professional and was the breadwinner for the family of three young
daughters.

I have to admit, as a career police officer, I'm skeptical
when spouses of drug dealers claim they had no clue what was
going on in their own houses, by a person they chose to marry
and spend the rest of their lives with. This is true especially with
someone as sharp as Staci. So I asked her some hard questions.

"During that time [prior to the drug raid], did you ever
suspect there was anything illegal going on?"

She said, "I didn't know that anything illegal was going on.
But I knew something was wrong, and one of the questions I did
ask was, 'Are you using drugs?' I also had to ask him, 'Are you
having an affair, are you an alcoholic, are you not happy with
me?' He was never around, and I wanted to know what was
going on.

"I have no doubt there are people who doubted me, who
said, 'How can this be going on under your nose and you don't
know that it's happening?' I absolutely understand that feeling
today."

I pressed Staci by asking her if, as a health professional and
being accomplished in the field, she noticed any signs with her
husband of methamphetamine.

"No," she said. "He didn't lose all his teeth, he didn't have
bad skin, he didn't lose a lot of weight. But something that I did
notice that I would be questioning today is he was so disengaged
from his family. He was absent as a parent, and I couldn't have
a conversation with him. If I started talking to him, he would
fall asleep. He missed a lot of important events. So personality
changes were significant."

She noted, "He could look me straight in the face and not
even blink and lie, and it was just so natural."

As their marriage progressed, and her husband's mental and physical state declined, there were other strains in their relationship.

"Oh, it was horrible, it was volatile. I would get so mad that I would hit him. He would spit in my face. And as far as intimacy, there was none. We really led separate lives."

Shortly after we met at the book-signing event, Staci agreed to sit down with me for an in-depth interview about the arrest of her husband, over fifteen years prior. During my interview I felt the urge to revert to when I was a cop, grilling a suspect by peppering them with the evidence we had until they would mentally break down and confess to the crime. But I realized the situation here was different.

During our time together, sitting on opposite sides of a table, Staci was not charged with a crime, and I was no longer a police officer. I had to let up on the gas pedal, which was tough for me to do. The cop in me still wanted to get the truth out of her.

I pointed out we had been investigating her husband for years, and that he was considered a large-scale dealer. We considered him so dangerous that I took a fully armed SWAT team to execute the search warrant on their house.

Besides the methamphetamine, we also discovered outside surveillance cameras hooked to monitors in the basement, microphones outside the exterior doors, and an arsenal of weapons and ammunition throughout the house.

"Staci, he had an assault rifle in your bedroom up against the wall."

"Wow" was her response.

I asked her how she didn't see the multiple monitors in the basement hooked up to cameras outside the house.

"Now my answer for that is maybe he didn't have the system on when I was downstairs," she said.

"Did you ever see guns around the house?"

"No, no."

"He had quite an arsenal."

"That blows me away, wow."

"That's scary with the kids obviously," I said.

"Oh, it's scary, period. What if some crazy person would have gotten into the house and killed us or something?"

WHAT ABOUT THAT OTHER WOMAN?

At this point in the interview I homed in on the most exciting and curious part of Staci's crazy story—the other woman hidden in Staci's very own house.

"Did you know about this room?"

"No."

"No idea this hidden room is there?"

"No."

"And had you seen this woman before?"

"I had. She's certainly not a personal friend of mine. We didn't run in the same social circles. She was someone I had met, and I knew who she was. She was dating a guy, and that's how I actually knew her. She never acted weird around me, never seemed like she was hiding anything from me. It just seemed like she was one of the guys, I guess."

"And what did your husband tell you about his relationship with this girl?"

"He told me that she was his connection to whoever he was buying drugs from. He denied there was a physical relationship with her. He told me, 'Staci, come on, my God, look at her! Do you really think I would be attracted to that?'"

I pointed out to Staci that in the hidden room with the girl we had found meth-smoking materials, a mattress, and mason jars full of urine.

"There was more than that" was Staci's reply, which certainly piqued my interest.

Staci had returned to the house hours after the raid had concluded and after her husband had been taken to jail, and she conducted an even more thorough search of the hidden room, finding items I had forgotten about.

"There was tons of pornographic materials and pornographic toys and mirrors all over. I smashed every mirror. I remember then thinking the man could have opened up his own Dr. John's shop [a popular sex toy shop in Omaha]. I thought, 'Geez, I hope I don't have something.'

"My neighbor was with me and I looked at her and said, 'Just look at this, this is such shit!' I was just furious. I was mad about everything."

I asked Staci if she suspected a sexual relationship between her husband and the hidden woman, and in true form she did not hold back.

"I definitely think he was fucking the worthless bitch, even though he swore up and down he was not in a sexual relationship with her. Why else would he be hiding her in this room? Unless he was using these sex toys on himself, there's no doubt in my mind he was screwing this disgusting mess. He certainly wasn't using these sex toys with me!"

Interestingly, Staci remained married to her husband during his three-year incarceration, even visiting him on a regular basis with their small daughters.

During his incarceration Staci said some of her husband's drug-dealing buddies started showing her attention never before displayed. "I think they wanted money, and I think they probably wanted sex."

In my career as a drug cop I never thought of career methamphetamine users and dealers as being the romantic types. But one did his best to get Staci's attention while her husband was rotting in a federal prison.

"Some idiot left a note in my door. He drew a picture of the sun and the note said, 'You are hot like the sun.' I just shredded it. I was so disgusted," she told me, with a subtle smile.

After her husband's release, Staci, her husband, and their three small daughters resumed their life in the same home in Omaha, minus the surveillance equipment, guns, and drugs.

After a year she filed for divorce.

"He had completely manipulated the children. I wasn't wearing my wedding ring, and it was very contentious. I really did not like him." But she just couldn't bring herself to finalize the divorce.

I have often wondered what attracts certain girls to bad guys. Why do they stay with them and put up with all the bullshit that goes with it? Many good girls over the years have told me they are attracted to the dangerous aspect of the relationship. Others feel that they are the only ones who can profoundly change him.

Whatever the case, I had a hard time dragging an answer out of Staci as to why she couldn't bring herself to sever ties with her husband.

"I just couldn't pull the trigger and that is my biggest regret. He turned out to be a royal pain in my ass and real problematic, because in the end he ended up divorcing *me*. Isn't that crazy?"

The last part of her statement caught me by surprise.

"Why did he file for divorce from you?"

"Well, while he was gone, I began an affair with a fellow health professional and that in itself was a horrible situation."

"Was that while he was in prison?"

"Yes."

"Did it continue after he got out of prison?"

"It did. He actually wanted me to marry him and I couldn't do that. I know he [her husband] was hurt by this. I know he was angry. He asked me about it, and I didn't deny it. I told him the truth."

Her husband told her, "I want you to stop seeing him."

"No, I won't, not going to do it."

Staci was actually divorced by her husband, the convicted drug dealer who put her and her daughters through a period of hell on earth.

We ended the interview on a poignant note. Sitting with Staci for several hours caused me to realize that even though I have my suspicions about her knowledge and involvement in that crazy life with her husband, I am not always right in my assumptions. She is an engaging, attractive, and insightful person.

I've decided to give her the benefit of the doubt, while realizing that I have been burned before.

Staci wanted to culminate the interview on several important notes.

Both of us were happy and relieved that she and her three daughters were not home when the SWAT team, led by me, deployed on their house. The loud percussion of stun grenades coupled with the intimidating, forceful entrance by the heavily armed officers would have been too much for the children to bear.

One vivid image Staci has, after she returned to her house, is of a SWAT officer playing with her dog who was there during the dynamic entry. The dog was most certainly scared to death.

"I'm so glad my dog wasn't hurt!"

Staci said her ex-husband is way behind on child support, and she has full plans to collect. "Yeah, I'm going to prove something to him. Vengeance is so golden."

One emotional aspect in Staci's mind is the toll all of this took on her father. "I remember after the raid he came over and cried. My dad does not show any emotion, so for him to be that hurt."

I responded, "When daughters are involved, it's a rough deal for dads."

Finally, I asked how her three daughters were doing, fifteen years after their lives were turned upside down as small kids. They still have a relationship with their father, who remains in the same house where the raid took place in 2001. All three seem to have turned the corner and have happy, productive lives.

"The day after the raid I was sitting on the couch with the girls and the media was camped outside the house. I remember my eight-year-old daughter looking at me crying, wringing her hands.

"'Mom,' she said to me, 'I think Dad did something really bad.'"

THE GUY

I recently contacted the husband and asked if he would allow me to interview him. I was not sure what type of reception I would receive, especially due to my portrayal of him as being a conniving, manipulative drug dealer.

I texted him, *This is Mark Langan. We met in passing awhile back and you mentioned the possibility of sitting down with me for my second book, to tell "the rest of the story." Are you willing? I hope so. Let me know. Thank you.*

Within minutes I received the response, *No, thank you.*

I was disappointed, since he sounded eager when I met him at a book-signing event a few months prior. I thought he could fill in a lot of the blanks about the dysfunctionality taking place in his house at the time of the bust.

So I pressed him by texting, *Ok. If you change your mind, please contact me. Thank you.*

Shortly he texted back: *I'm sorry, but I won't. Good luck and I hope it does well Mark. Thank you for your service too.*

Times change. People change.

16

WHY DO SOME GIRLS LIKE THE BAD BOYS?

was at an extremely busy event selling my first book. The place was packed with patrons, and I was signing one book after another.

I barely noticed the attractive, midtwenties woman who was standing behind my table. She had coal black, long hair, a white pullover top that left little to the imagination, and skin-tight white leggings. She was standing in a spot behind me that made me a bit uncomfortable, so I stood up and asked her what she was doing.

"Can you help me?" she asked.

I noticed her eyes were glazed over, and her breath almost knocked me over from the pungent smell of smoking methamphetamine.

"My boyfriend is trying to find me, and he's going to hurt me," she said, adding, "please hide me right now."

She was frantic and shaking. There was another young woman who was assisting me with the book sales, and I could tell by the look on her face that she was scared by what the drug-induced girl was telling me.

I told her to calm down, and that I would call the police for her.

"No, no, I don't want the police. Just hide me now, please!" she said, her voice increasing with urgency.

She tried to hide behind our book display, toward the back of our booth. I was scared she was going to knock stuff over, causing the bookshelves to collapse.

I asked what her boyfriend's name was, and she looked at me with an eerily frightening glare, refusing to tell me.

"Just take me with you now, I want to leave with you," she said over and over. I knew the last thing I should do is leave in my car with this vulnerable female. This was not an option.

"Okay then," she said, after being told we were not going anywhere, "let me use your phone to call my mother."

This also was not an option, as I was not going to let her use my personal phone to call God knows whoever. I told her there was security at the event, and I would take her to meet them so she would be safe.

As I started walking out of my booth area, I saw a guy rapidly approaching and locked eyes with presumably the boyfriend she was scared to death of. He was walking toward us, with an intent stare and a purposeful gait—a man on a mission. The guy was in his forties, wearing a tight shirt that showed off his impressive physique.

I'm thinking, the last thing I want is a physical altercation between these two, where I needed to step in and protect this girl.

All I wanted to do was sell books.

The boyfriend walked up to my booth and without hesitating extended his hand and said, "Hello, Mr. Langan, how are you today?"

It turns out I had arrested this guy well before I retired, for selling drugs and possessing weapons. He was a notorious, dangerous gangbanger who had quite the reputation on the street as being an enforcer who stopped at nothing to collect his drug debts. My crew had put him away for an extended stretch, and I had not thought of him in many years.

Miguel (not his real name) had also played the game of snitching his friends off. We made a few good arrests from the information he supplied, most likely resulting in a few years shaved off his prison sentence.

Obviously, he remembered me.

I engaged him in small talk to try to defuse this potentially volatile situation. He told me he turned his life around, was clean, and living a lawful lifestyle. He told me he had previously bought and read my book, so I thought he couldn't be all bad.

"Why am I not in your book?" he asked while laughing nervously, darting from my eyes to his girlfriend in my booth.

All during the conversation the girl did not budge from behind my table. She was silent and still had that panicked look on her face.

Suddenly, he turned to her and said, "Let's go, babe."

Then an awkward silence.

I looked at her, she looked at him, he looked at me, and we kept looking each other over for what seemed like a full minute when it was probably only ten seconds.

"What are you doing, let's go!" he said, with some frustration and urgency in his voice. He raised his left hand and motioned condescendingly with his fingers, like gesturing a dog to come into the house.

I decided it was time to make my move. "Miguel, we need to talk. Let's take a walk outside."

With that he walked with me out the exit of the venue and asked what was going on.

"Miguel, I'm not a cop anymore, so you don't have to listen to anything I say. But I'm telling you, this girl is high as a kite and scared to death of you. She does not want to go with you because she thinks you will hurt her."

Miguel started protesting, and I stopped him midsentence.

"If you create a scene or try to take her forcibly, I will call the police and do my best to prevent that from happening until they get here."

He looked me over for a few seconds, took a breath, and said, "Mark, you were always a square-shooter with me, so I'm not going to cause you any problems. Besides, this bitch just caught me cheating on her and now she's freaking out. I'm done with this fucking bitch. I'm just going to leave."

With that I told Miguel he was making the right decision, wished him luck, and shook his hand. He walked away muttering to himself and shaking his head.

The girlfriend was still near my booth when I returned, and shortly thereafter the police were called and whisked her away, presumably to a safe location. I remember wondering to myself how soon she would reunite herself with Miguel, and if she was in fact later harmed either physically or mentally. Miguel could not have been an easy guy to have a stable relationship with.

"I LOVE THE DANGER"

Afterward I pondered two thoughts.

First, why did she pick me out from thousands of people to hide behind? There was no indication she knew me or my past profession. Or did the title of my book, *Busting Bad Guys*, prominently displayed at my table tell her this was an area where she could feel safe?

Second, I asked myself the same question that rattled through my mind for years on the Omaha Police Department.

Why would a beautiful young girl like her start a relationship with a hardened criminal, twenty years her senior, a guy who at one point in his life was an extremely dangerous individual who surrounded himself with guns and drugs?

I remember frequently asking this very question of many similar young girls I dealt with while a police officer. The answers were usually similar.

Many of the girls felt they could change the degenerate criminal they were dating. They felt they could provide the recipe for him to turn his life around, while at the same time he had them selling drugs and prostituting themselves.

These girls were too naïve to realize that they were but a piece of property to these guys, property that could be discarded at a second's notice. These men did not love them. In fact, they loved nobody but themselves.

But these girls were convinced they could change the guy into becoming something that was impossible to achieve. I usually tried to get these girls as much help as I could. Their self-esteem was so low, and they were so strung out on drugs that, if I didn't help them, I was not sure who would.

The other answer I received about the draw to low-life boyfriends was even more concerning.

"I love the danger" would be an all-too-often answer the sweet young teen would tell me about her piece-of-crap boyfriend. They were excited about the thrill of the drug dealing, easy money, and free-wheeling sexcapades. These girls were most likely beyond repair, and I could do little to help them out of the lifestyle.

Several months later I read in the *Omaha World-Herald* that Miguel had been arrested for kidnapping and false imprisonment. I later verified that his crime involved the same young girl who had sought me out for protection. The article talked of the injuries he caused the victim while holding her captive for several days.

About a year later, while working at the Nebraska Humane Society, I received a letter from Miguel, begging me for help. Even though I had been retired from law enforcement for over ten years, Miguel still felt that I was his meal ticket for a reduced sentence, or even probation.

He started his handwritten note by saying, "Dear Mark, I want to cut a deal with the federal government. I couldn't think of anyone else to contact. I helped you in 1999 and got you some very nice and easy targets. I did have to testify on the stand but it's all good. I was disgusted back then about snitching or testifying against anyone. That is no longer the case."

His note went on, "I can make one fucking call and get one or two pounds of meth delivered on a silver platter! I'm going on 40 now and believe me, I can deliver a 50 pound bust off a Sinaloa cartel member I have met here in jail. If I do this, I want immunity, a new identity, and 100k. The OPD [Omaha Police Department] and FBI are busting bottom feeders. Let me know if your [sic] interested or can send someone to see me with some pull to strike a deal."

I chuckled as I read his note. Did he seriously think I was going to try to get him out of jail for assaulting that girl and holding her captive? Even if I wanted to, did he think I had the power to do so? His note held no credibility with me.

He ended the note by telling me, "When I was a kid, I loved playing cops and robbers. I always chose to be the cop. I was damn good too."

Miguel is currently rotting in a prison cell and is not due to see the light of day for thirty some odd years. I will be ninety-two years old when he gets out.

I hope the young girl he beat, and got hooked onto meth-amphetamine, is happy and healthy. Most importantly, I hope she is staying away from bad boys.

THE HAPPIER PART OF PROMOTING MY BOOKS

Not all the notes I get are pleas to help the bad guys. Here is one that makes my work all worthwhile. Some girls do get away from the bad boys.

10·22·01

Officer Langan,

I do not want to take
up your time, but I have
wanted to write this for so
long. I lost your card so
I called to see where to
send this. I am, because
if you able to look people
in the eye again, pay my
bills, have a good family, home
life, be close to my parents and
children, have real friends
and respect myself and be
honest with myself and everyone
else. I am now happily married
and am no longer in the ██████
business. I have a decent job
I look forward to everyday.
Because of you I am no
longer on drugs. I wanted you
to know these things because
whether or not you ever
wonder about the people you
come into contact with, you
do make a wonderful difference
or at least you did in my
life.
                    Very truly yours,
██████████████████████

The part of promoting my books I find the most enjoyable
is when people come up to me at a book-signing event or see
me in a crowd and say how they've turned their lives around
after being arrested by myself or my crew of narcotics officers. It
never gets old.

I was talking to a university class in the spring of 2014 about my career with the Omaha Police Department and about my book.

I was telling the young adults about the lives we changed both for the better and, in some situations, for the worse. I could see the students were transfixed with my stories of undercover drug buys, wiretaps, and chasing bad guys down dark alleys in the wee hours of the night.

One girl, in her early twenties, raised her hand and asked, "So are you saying it's impactful for you when a person changes their life for the better, due to you having arrested them?"

"Yes," I responded, "it's especially important for me to know that all my work wasn't in vain."

"Okay, well, you arrested my mother fifteen years ago for selling cocaine," she said. "She got out of prison five years ago. She's now a drug counselor and frequently talks about how you saved her life by arresting her when you did."

The girl continued, "I told her you were talking to us tonight, and she wanted me to say hello and thanks to you. So that's what I'm doing."

How gutsy was it for this young woman to bare her life, and her mother's, to her fellow students? The girl had tears in her eyes as I looked at her, and I told her how much this meant to me. I did not ask the mother's name, as I figured she would have told me if she wanted to.

The name wasn't nearly as important as the message.

17

YOUR DAUGHTER IS CALLING

A few years ago, I was invited to attend a luncheon for a group of aspiring young leaders working their way through the ranks of prominent Omaha businesses, ranging from nonprofits to *Fortune* 500 mega-companies.

These bright men and women were part of Leadership Omaha, formed in 1978 by the Greater Omaha Chamber of Commerce to develop effective leaders who strengthen and transform both their businesses and their community.

The student leaders devoted much time to satisfying the requirements for graduation from this prestigious program. I was honored to be asked to attend their luncheon, and I certainly was never one to turn down a networking lunch and a way to promote my new job at the Nebraska Humane Society.

I figured the keynote speaker would be the CEO of a major company, or an Omaha-based entrepreneur who made millions of dollars based on an outside-the-box idea.

Someone pointed out the keynote speaker sitting at the head table. I was surprised to see that he was dressed inappropriately for the event, wearing a simple shirt and wrinkled khaki pants. Everyone else wore business attire. He was a middle-aged white guy, unshaven, with a mustache that needed trimming. It was obvious he was socially awkward, given that he stared at his plate of food while those around him carried on hearty conversations.

He also looked familiar, and I couldn't take my eyes off him. Did I personally know him, or did I recognize his odd behavior as being reminiscent of the lost souls that became such a large part of my previous life?

After all, I had retired after twenty-six years as an Omaha Police officer—most notably, as a sergeant on the narcotics squad. My team would bust down doors and arrest bad guys, usually methamphetamine users and dealers. Of all the drugs we arrested people for selling, meth sucked the souls out of innocent kids whose parents spent their days tweaking on the devil's pipe while ignoring even the basic needs of their young children.

Those blameless kids tore my heart out every time we splintered a door and found a little boy or girl in the midst of a filthy drug-strewn living room. One little girl still haunts my thoughts. She clung to my leg and cried, "Please don't let anybody hurt me anymore."

The keynote speaker was introduced by a young professional who talked of volunteering his time at a substance abuse facility where he met this guy. Then things were making sense to me, and I was anxious for the keynoter to get up and talk.

The introducer set up the speaker by saying he had an inspirational story to tell us, and that in his case, hard work and dedication (like that of these young professionals) paid off in his life.

With that, the speaker was officially introduced, the crowd began politely clapping, and he hesitantly approached the microphone.

"I am a recovering methamphetamine addict, and many times I have spiraled downward, almost to the point of no return," his voice barely audible even with a microphone. In fact, his sponsor nudged him to talk louder.

"Methamphetamine is the devil's drug, and I was ruled by the devil for many years. I lost my wife, my family, my money," he went on. "I wanted nothing in life except for my next high. I had no goals, no job, and I did whatever it took to survive day-to-day."

The crowd was attentive, with most of the attendees never actually having heard from a person like this. His story was, sadly, all too familiar to me.

"About a year ago I was always high. I was a recluse in my house, with the windows and blinds closed. I never answered the door and wanted nothing to do with friends, neighbors, or even my own kids. I had hit rock bottom," he admitted to the group.

"One afternoon the phone rang, and I saw on the caller ID that it was my daughter calling. I'd been lying to her for years, telling her I was off the stuff and doing good. Meth addicts are great at lying, even to their own kids."

The crowd was quiet, transfixed now on the meth addict at the podium revealing a real-life episode of *Breaking Bad*.

"I decided to answer the phone even though I didn't want to. You see, even though I was high, and just wanted to be left alone, I knew in my mind that, as a dad, if my daughter is calling for me, I must answer her call."

The words began resonating with me as I sat there. As a father of a daughter, I understood exactly what he was saying.

"So I answered the phone, and my daughter could immediately tell I was high. She started crying and asked me why I kept doing this to myself," he said.

"'I love you, Dad,' she said. 'Let me help you. Please! I don't want to lose you!'"

The guy then choked up at the microphone and had to compose himself. The crowd was eerily silent, with lumps forming in my throat and in the throats of others in the crowd.

"That was the call that changed my life," he said.

Soon after the call from his daughter, the guy entered substance abuse rehabilitation. A year later found him here, speaking in front of three hundred professionals, most of whom had never seen methamphetamine.

Fast-forward a couple of years. My own daughter was now a college graduate who had earned the title of Doctor of Pharmacy. I felt strongly about telling her the story of the drug addict who loved his daughter so much that he was forced to make a life-altering decision.

I told my daughter about his story of lifelong drug abuse, leading to the life-changing phone call from his daughter.

"Katie," I told her, "I am so proud of you and all your achievements. I have no doubt you can take care of yourself. But I have to say, as your father, that if I'm ever in an important meeting, at a movie, or just in a mood where I don't want to be bothered, and I see your name on the caller ID of my cell phone, I will *always* answer your call, no matter what I'm doing."

I said, "I will always be there for you, because that's what fathers do."

With that, Katie gave me a hug and kiss on the cheek, and I realized it was a moment I would cherish forever.

This was not easy for me. I have never been one to show my emotions, even with my own family. Though, with my lone daughter, I should never be scared to reveal what I am thinking, what matters to me, and why I love her.

In that respect I need to be a better father.

I do not remember the guy's name who told his story. I still don't know why he looked familiar. Maybe I arrested him. Maybe not.

But I hope he is doing well and, most importantly, still answering his daughter's phone calls.

18

THE OTHER DAUGHTER REVISITED

On Valentine's Day 2002, Officer Gary Kula and I shot and killed thirty-seven-year-old Jose Chavez near the intersection of 28th and Madison in South Omaha—a working-class neighborhood of mostly small one-story homes overshadowed by massive mature trees, with plenty of cars parked along narrow streets with wide sidewalks.

And so began my first book.

Why do I drive down that South Omaha street when I'm in the area? Why do I wonder if I could have done things better, such as not allowing the suspect to fire on us first before we had to kill him?

Was I watching his hands like I was trained to do? Just how close did I come to losing an officer that night?

I believe something good always comes from something bad. No matter how sad or gut wrenching a situation may be (and I have experienced plenty), I have been able to extract positives that help me deal with future similar types of calamity.

The fact I was able to connect with the daughter of the man I shot (and who ultimately died) has been an important healing aspect for me. It is a rare relationship indeed between a young lady and the man who killed her father.

After my first book was published, I received a beautifully written email from the daughter of our suspect, who critiqued the chapters I wrote about both her father and subsequent meeting I had with her. I will share her email with you, but first, some thoughts about officer-involved shootings.

VALENTINE'S DAY 2002

The chance a police officer will ever shoot and kill someone is remote. Yet, there I was eighteen years ago, standing in the middle of a dark, silent street in the chilly winter weather, shooting at a bad guy who was trying to kill one of my officers.

Those few seconds have left a lasting impression on me, well into my retirement. Why was I one of "those officers"—the less than five-percenters who was forced to kill someone?

I have always denied experiencing any type of posttraumatic stress, yet there are times I wonder why I think about that night every day.

I cannot begin to count the number of armed drug dealers my crew had arrested up to this fateful night. We had chased armed suspects through dark yards, knocked down motel room doors, found perps on beds next to semi-automatic rifles, and were fired upon by a sniper while serving a crack warrant in 1992.

The odds were bound to catch up to us sooner or later that someone—either a member of my crew or I—would be involved in a shooting where one of us, or the suspect, would be killed or seriously injured.

Yet the chances of police officers using their firearms to kill someone are remote at best. There are close to a million cops in the United States, with an average of three hundred fatal shootings a year by police officers.

Bad guys shoot cops too. I sure never wanted to be one of them, but standing in the street that night, the thought crossed my mind.

Ironically, in the past ten years the most officer-involved shootings have occurred on a Thursday. What is the significance of Thursday for violence toward police officers? I have no clue, but February 14, 2002, was a Thursday.

This particular day started out no differently than all the others, but it ended up being a defining moment for my fellow officer Gary Kula's career and mine. We shot a man, a suspected drug dealer who fired at us. We fired back. He died on the street.

THE AFTERMATH

Several years after my retirement from the Omaha Police Department, while I was at work at the Nebraska Humane Society, most likely poring over dog bite reports or dealing with any number of frustrated citizens, upset over the handling of their neighbor's barking dog or the family of rabbits eating their prized homegrown vegetables, my phone rang.

"This is Mark Langan," I answered, waiting for the next challenge coming my way.

A soft-voiced young lady, whose tone was so meek and mild that I could barely hear her, said, "I am the daughter of Jose Chavez, the man you and Officer Kula shot several years ago."

I paused, not knowing what to say. I was apprehensive to talk to this young lady. I had no idea why she was calling me, what she wanted, or even if I was being tape-recorded for legal reasons, anticipating a future lawsuit.

I immediately thought I'd better be careful how I handled this situation.

The daughter sensed my heightened concern and said, "Mr. Langan, I want to assure you that I pose no danger and have no ill will toward you or Officer Kula. I'd just like to talk and ask you for a favor."

Her calming tone immediately put me at ease. Yet I still did not know who she was or the motive for this telephone call.

However, something told me not to hang up, and not to dismiss her as a lunatic caller who simply wanted to exploit this time to rehash the officer-involved shooting death of her father to further her own agenda.

Rather, I stayed with her on the phone and told her I was willing to listen. I offered little in the area of conversation and made it clear that the ball was in her court. I was willing to give her some limited time to talk to me.

I learned she was a young woman in her early twenties, working toward a degree at a small Midwestern university. I was surprised when she told me this, as years of being a cynical cop did not prepare me to believe that the daughter of Jose Chavez might actually be a college student who happened to have lost her father in a violent encounter with the police.

She made it known during the call that she was a spiritual person, and her faith in God had led her to call me this day.

Sadly, I had given little thought to Chavez's family after the shooting investigation and grand jury finally ended. During this phone call I realized it was now time to listen to his daughter, who obviously had a serious reason to reach out to me three years after I had shot and killed her father.

The conversation continued to be one-sided, with the quiet, somewhat monotone voice of this girl dominating the conversation. She talked like the nuns that taught me at Blessed Sacrament School, with a soothing cadence that immediately put me at ease just like Sister Julie Ann did when I would become upset or frustrated in first grade.

"Mr. Langan, I have a big favor to ask of you, and I'm hoping you will grant me my wish. Will you and Officer Kula meet with me so I can ask you some questions about what happened to my father that night and why it had to happen?"

Wow. This was a telephone call out of the blue. I never would have thought in a million years the daughter of Jose Chavez would want to meet with me and talk about her father's death.

I didn't know what to say so I handled her call just like many others that presented challenges to me. I told her, "Please give me your number, and I promise to call you back."

I needed some time to absorb this telephone call and to also call Gary Kula to get his take on the daughter's request. I had every intention of calling her back with whatever we decided. I just needed time to think.

"Thank you and I look forward to your call," she politely said.

Within minutes I was on the phone with Gary, and he was as surprised as I was that Chavez's daughter had reached out to me.

Gary was always savvy about dealing with complicated issues head on, which is why he performed so well while assigned to my narcotics unit crew. After several minutes of talking it over, Gary said, "I say we meet with her in a public place and see what she wants to talk about."

I agreed with Gary. Not meeting with the daughter would have been a sign of weakness on our parts. After all, we had nothing to hide because both of us had been successfully vetted in the Chavez shooting.

If things got out of hand with her, we would simply walk away. I wanted to give this girl a chance to meet with us, since her demeanor on the phone told me how important this meeting was to her.

We decided to meet her in a busy restaurant in midtown Omaha, around two in the afternoon. We completed a background check on her and even though nothing in her past caused us any concern for our safety, we did have covert police security in the restaurant in case she became violent and tried to shoot or stab us.

As soon as we entered the restaurant, I recognized her standing alone, obviously waiting for someone. She was in her early twenties, with short dark hair and being of Hispanic descent. I could immediately see signs of her father's eyes when looking at her facial features. As soon as our eyes met, we walked to each other and uncomfortably shook hands, exchanging pleasantries before the three of us sat at a table.

Immediately she thanked us for meeting her. I could tell she was already emotional, with tears not far behind her bloodshot eyes. Most likely she had been crying before she entered the restaurant in anticipation of meeting with Gary and me.

"I want to start by saying that I forgive you for killing my father," she said softly.

Gary or I could have responded in a couple of ways. First, there was no reason to forgive us because we had done nothing wrong. Or, as we chose, we thanked her for her kindness. We certainly did not want to exasperate this stressful situation by arguing with her on the idea of whether forgiveness was necessary or appropriate.

To her, the forgiveness was sincere. That was all that mattered at the time.

This girl had no malice in her soul, and Gary and I took this into account during our talk. To her this was a meeting of utmost importance, and we owed her our undivided attention.

"I have one important question for both of you, one that has bothered me since my father died," she said.

Gary and I were all ears, glancing at each other periodically as a form of mental reassurance that we were there for each other.

"Did either of you have any other choice but to shoot and kill my father?" she asked, dissolving into tears once she finished the question.

Other customers were now watching us, as Jose Chavez's daughter was audibly sobbing once she had asked the question she had waited three years to ask.

"No, we had no choice," I answered, trying to appear as human as possible and certainly not wanting to come across as an uncaring cop. "We had no choice because your father pulled a gun out and shot at Officer Kula, trying to kill him." I hoped my words were not too strong for her to absorb.

Gary also assured her that we wish the entire incident had never happened.

I finished by saying, "If I could go back in time and prevent this from happening, I would. But your father made a choice that night, and all our lives have changed because of his decision." I wanted her to realize how the shooting death of her father had affected Gary and me also.

She said she understood and went on to tell us how her family has been suffering since that fateful night. At the end of our brief meeting together, she asked if we could all hold hands and pray. I was a bit self-conscious doing this in a packed restaurant, but I decided to let my guard down and roll with the flow.

As we all held hands, she said a silent prayer, closing her eyes and mumbling the words that were ever so important to her at that time.

We then released hands and stood up. She thanked us and walked away.

The shooting death of her father had been devastating to her family in ways that I never took time to consider. I realized that besides being a violent gunman that night, Jose Chavez was also a family man who had a wife and four daughters who loved him.

His daughter had maintained her spirituality throughout the ordeal. Her belief in God had guided her through the rough times, leading her to this meeting with Gary and me.

I will never forget it.

GARY KULA REMEMBERS THAT NIGHT

The shooting of Jose Chavez on the night of February 14, 2002, changed many lives and ended another. His decision to pull the trigger of his revolver not only brought great pain to his family, it also caused me to never look at life the same way again. I realized just moments after the smoke of the gunpowder had cleared, my life had changed forever.

Gone was my sense of invincibility and cop bravado of thinking I couldn't be hurt. As the blood of Chavez spilled onto the street, the thrill of working narcotics cases, busting down doors, and chasing dopers down went away.

As the days, months, and years go by, I think about that night less often. But the emotions and feelings I have regarding the shooting quickly come pouring back to the forefront of my mind from time to time. It happens when similar shootings occur with police officers.

I'm certainly grateful for making it out alive and not hurting physically. Emotionally, who knows. I'm also grateful for the love and support I received from family, friends, my pastor Father Don, fellow officers, and the oldest daughter of Chavez. She helped me get closure and a sense of peace knowing someone in his family had come to terms with what had happened.

ANOTHER CHAPTER IN THIS TRAGEDY

Shortly after my first book came out and after our meeting with the daughter of the shooting victim, I received this email from her, the daughter of Jose Chavez, whom I have chosen not to name.

Mark,

I hope this message finds you in good spirits. I sincerely hope I'm not putting a damper on your book release cheer. I'm sorry for the lengthy message, my emails can get a little out of control.

I wanted to acknowledge I've read the main chapters concerning my father's case.

I'm still processing what I read, I haven't completely absorbed it, there's a lot to take in. It's hard to describe but the experience reminded me of my bad habit of reading the endings of books and then going back to the beginning to read how the story unfolded the way it did. With this, it kind of felt like that—I know the ending, my dad dies and that's it, or at least that's it for him, not for the rest of us.

I trust you know I'm reading it in good faith and assuming everything to be true and accurate…. It's not easy to read that your dad tried to kill a cop, it's pretty devastating.

In any case, it might be too soon for me to say, but I might actually end up being thankful you wrote the book for whatever that is worth.

While it feels like I'm in the front row watching him die reading your words over and over again, which is a very painful experience, I at least have a better idea of the events and decisions leading up to his death.

Regarding me, I have no regrets in reaching out to you, Gary or Pam, then or now. [Pam was a third officer involved in the shooting.] I did find it humorous that there was a background check performed and covert surveillance in place, it was the only time I laughed reading it, but I understand the concern for your safety. I still appreciate that you all took the time to meet with me, I can appreciate how unusual my request must have come across but I am grateful you took a chance on me. I constantly review my reasons for contacting you, one of which is my commitment to live my life in a way that honors all the good decisions my father made, to show you that he was more than what you experienced that night. I don't want people to assume he was a "bad" man, if he was I wouldn't have grown into the woman I am today. It upsets me and my family that he was reduced to the label of "drug-dealer" but that was inevitable given the circumstances and cannot be helped (I'm grateful it wasn't "cop killer" because that would have been awful to live with).... He made sacrifices for me and my sisters that I will never understand because I am not a father. As you've witnessed through other cases you worked, my life could have turned out much differently had my father not emphasized the importance of getting an education and staying away from drugs and alcohol.

As to forgiveness, as I acknowledged last September, I'm sorry if I came across as presumptuous at Village Inn, I'd already arrived at that conclusion myself. It was certainly not my intention to come across as judge and jury or imply you had done something "wrong." It's complicated, I still don't think I can articulate it fully, it's something I have to work on every day, I realize "forgiveness" is a fluid and holistic term. I meant to convey that at least one of us was not angry and that I did not hold you responsible for doing what you had to do that night, that I didn't blame you for how my family's lives unfolded after that night. Those "words" I mumbled when we held hands, I can't explain why it was very important to hold the hands that pulled the trigger that ended my father's life, I was praying the "Our Father." I lingered over the line "forgive us our trespasses as we forgive those who trespass against us," I take that line pretty seriously. Again, I really do not blame you for the position you were in that night but as I'm sure you realized it was more about me than it was about you. I was very angry with my father when he died over something childish and it hurts to know that he died thinking I was mad at him or that I didn't love him anymore. "Forgiving" you was more about forgiving myself for being a typical, angry teenager and forgiving that young girl. Maybe even forgiving him for making the wrong decision that night and leaving us alone. I would have preferred he had served out a prison term or faced deportation, at least he'd be alive rather than lost to us forever. While I didn't have a chance to say good-bye to him, it felt like I had a chance to do so through you. At that time, I really needed you to know that I was not angry anymore, meeting all of you helped me see that you were human beings with families and loved ones too with full lives to live. People with feelings who were also affected by what happened.

I will always wonder "why" and I'll never get an answer. And what I said at Village Inn remains true today, while I grieve my father's loss every day, how can I not when I only have to look in a mirror and see his face staring back at me, I am glad he did not hurt or kill any of you that night. I would not have wanted that pain for your respective families.

I will always feel a connection with this young woman. The thirty-two shots fired in thirteen seconds on February 14, 2002, changed lives forever.

19

THE CASE FOR (OR MAYBE AGAINST) THE DEATH PENALTY

Monsters walk the streets of Omaha, preying on the most vulnerable victims society has to offer. The idea of a child being viciously killed at the hands of a murderer turns my gut inside out. Or a young and vibrant mother being ripped from her car and shot in the head, while having mere seconds to realize she will never see her kids again.

Sadly, there have been multiple kids and adults from Omaha who have died gruesome deaths at the hands of demons. There are too many innocents who, in the blink of an eye, had their lives torn from them.

Up until the last few years I did not struggle with the idea of the State of Nebraska taking the life from a person who, through all faults of their own, committed the most violent and heinous crimes.

After all, I have been a cop most of my life. Cops are predisposed to support the death penalty. We are wired to form quick judgments on those who menace society through violent behavior.

Cops have little if any sympathy for the gangbanger who killed multiple people during a drive-by shooting. Or for the young man who viciously stabbed his girlfriend and hid the body, never to be found.

I write this chapter to help better understand my position on when we pull the switch to electrocute an inmate or stick a needle in his arm.

Is it worse punishment forcing a person to live the rest of his life in a stinky, cramped prison cell with a three-hundred-pound "cellie" who has the word *HATER* tattooed across his forehead and who shits three feet in front of him twice a day?

Some recent Omaha cases stick out in my mind as we consider this issue: What is the best punishment for premeditated murder? What cases demand the execution of a cold-blooded killer?

HAUNTING MY THOUGHTS

In May 2015, Roberto C. Martinez-Marinero was twenty-five years old when he viciously stabbed his mother over twenty times in the face and torso and then beat her with a baseball bat.

After he killed forty-five-year-old Jesus Ismenia Marinero, he and his girlfriend, Gabriela Guevara, wrapped the corpse in a blanket and carried it from the house to a car. Martinez-Marinero then drove to a secluded area of southeast Omaha and dumped his mother like a piece of garbage.

It was later learned that Martinez-Marinero and his mother had an argument over money. Their words became heated, causing him to snap.

As if this wasn't bad enough, Martinez-Marinero made the fateful decision that two potential witnesses to the murder had to be eliminated.

His four-year-old half-brother, Josue, and eleven-month-old half-brother, Angel, were seen by Martinez-Marinero as threats to his freedom. In his sick and demented mind, he hatched a plan to eliminate the threats these babies posed, while hoping he and his girlfriend could return to their normal lives while most likely spending his mother's hard-earned money.

Apparently, he did not consider how obvious it would be that three members of his family had suddenly gone missing.

Martinez-Marinero decided he must kill four-year-old Josue. But first, he chose to simply dump baby Angel in a trash dumpster, miles away from the crime scene. Still alive, the baby experienced certain death if the dumpster was picked up and compressed in the trash truck the next day. Luckily, a passerby heard Angel whimpering in the dumpster and saved him from an excruciating demise.

Martinez-Marinero then took Josue on a long, dark drive to a spot in rural Douglas County, Nebraska. What was Josue thinking at the time? It was late at night, so hopefully he was asleep, totally oblivious to the violence that had occurred earlier. Or was he talkative to his older brother, asking where his mommy and baby brother were? Worst of all, I've asked myself for years, if he was scared and crying.

Sadly, while researching this story, I received my answer.

The car came to a stop on the West Center Street bridge located above the dark and muddy Elkhorn River. The investigation shows that Josue was crying and screaming as Martinez-Marinero forcibly pulled him from the car seat. Without hesitating, the older brother tossed Josue off the bridge to the water below. The boy hit the water after a ten- to fifteen-foot fall and was pulled down the river by the swift current.

My God, I cannot get the child's final thoughts out of my head.

Josue's body was found four days later, tangled in trees over a mile south of the West Center Street bridge.

The autopsy confirmed the four-year-old died from drowning. He was conscious and alert when his bother tossed him from the dark, desolate bridge into the Elkhorn River.

Josue Ramirez-Marinero, victim of a brutal homicide at the hands of his older brother, Roberto C. Martinez-Marinero.

Josue died a horrific death.

The investigation showed that Martinez-Marinero drove over twenty minutes with poor little Josue in the backseat. He had plenty of time to decide if he would spare his half-brother or kill him.

Martinez-Marinero made the premeditated decision to kill his little brother by tossing him from the bridge and drowning him.

He was quickly arrested after the double murders occurred, and he confessed to police.

Douglas County Attorney Don Kleine, who is well-respected by prosecutors and defense attorneys alike, allowed Martinez-Marinero to plead to first-degree murder. In exchange for the plea, he was spared the death penalty and instead was sentenced to a term of life without the possibility of parole.

The sentencing hearing was emotional, with family members asking the question that haunted them since the crime occurred. "I want to know, Roberto, why did you do it?" an aunt, Reina Marinero, asked, according to an *Omaha World-Herald* article.

Roberto C. Martinez-Marinero being escorted in the
Douglas County Courthouse in Omaha, 2016.
(Reprinted with permission of the Omaha World-Herald.*)*

Sadly, the defendant refused to acknowledge the question, or even his own family. He stood silent, continuing to be a coward.

"This pain will last for the rest of my life," Reina Marinero told the judge. "I will never be able to forgive him. Not till God tells me to."

The *Omaha World-Herald* further reported that Don Kleine (the prosecutor) choked back emotion. "Whenever you talk about these kinds of cases, they're very emotional," Kleine said, catching himself. "It's just draining when you think about the last moments of that little boy's life—and his mother's life."

The prosecutor said, "The thought process [Martinez-Marinero] had—some things you try and analyze, you try and figure out, you try to understand. And sometimes, it's impossible."

Roberto Martinez-Marinero was sentenced to two life sentences and is currently housed in the Nebraska Department of Corrections.

Should he have been given the death penalty? Lethal injection?

How about this next monster who stalked the streets?

A SERIAL MONSTER

Nikko Jenkins was born in 1986 and spent most of his early life in Omaha. He is one of the most well-known serial killers in the history of the city.

In 2013, Jenkins killed four people in just a matter of weeks.

The murders occurred within a month after he had been released from prison after serving ten and a half years of the twenty-one years to which he had been sentenced for a carjacking committed at age fifteen and for assaults committed in prison.

Jenkins was first arrested at the age of seven after he brought a loaded .25-caliber handgun to his school. When he was eleven, he stopped attending school, and his violence-prone lifestyle took hold. At age thirteen Jenkins had committed numerous assaults, including one with a knife.

Jenkins was sent to prison in 2003 for two armed carjackings, after spending time in a youth detention facility. While incarcerated, he was charged twice: for his part in a 2006 prison riot, as well as for assaulting a prison guard while on a furlough for his grandmother's funeral.

On July 30, 2013, Jenkins was released from the Nebraska Department of Corrections.

Soon, his family held a welcome-home party at a local Omaha motel. While there, an acquaintance of Nikko Jenkins gave him a twelve-gauge pistol grip shotgun as a gift.

Eleven days later Jenkins shot and killed Juan Uribe-Pena and Jorge C. Cajiga-Ruiz while they sat in a pickup truck in a dark, secluded parking lot in Spring Lake Park in South Omaha. Two female conspirators, including Jenkins's sister Erica, lured the victims to the spot with a promise of sex for money.

Instead of their receiving a good time, Nikko Jenkins ambushed them and shot both in the head. The motive appears to be robbery, as both victims' pockets were turned inside out.

Jenkins shot and killed Curtis Bradford in North Omaha on August 19, 2013, eight days after the shooting deaths of Uribe-Pena and Cajiga-Ruiz. Jenkins and Bradford met in prison and reconnected on the outside while plotting crimes known as *licks*—a street term for robbing random citizens and jacking their cars.

Bradford and Jenkins were seen together the day before the murder and even posed for a Facebook photograph. Bradford had been shot several times in his head and was found by a pass-erby in the parking lot of a housing complex.

Nikko Jenkins (left) and Curtis Bradford, shortly before Jenkins shot and killed Bradford. (Printed with permission of the Omaha Police Department.)

The murder of Curtis Bradford was hatched by both Nikko Jenkins and his sister Erica. The motive most likely was gang related. News accounts from the *Omaha World-Herald* show that Erica "yelled at her brother, Nikko Jenkins, for also firing into Bradford's head" and "taking my first kill."

Then, two days after the Bradford homicide, on August 21, 2013, Nikko Jenkins and his family of accomplices committed the murder that shook Omaha to its core.

Andrea Kruger was a thirty-three-year-old mother of three who tended bar at a popular West Omaha spot. Described by many as being vivacious and outgoing, Andrea was a hard worker who enjoyed talking to her customers and making them feel special. That summer night, she was returning home around 2:00 a.m. after closing the bar. She was hungry and decided to stop for a burger and drink from a northwest Omaha McDonald's.

Her decision to pull into that drive-through lane would cost Andrea her life.

Nikko Jenkins was on the prowl to do a lick. He, his sister Erica, their uncle Warren Levering, and cousin Christine Bordeaux were scoping for an easy target to rob and carjack.

They spotted Andrea in her Chevrolet Traverse. She was alone and a female, which in their sick minds made for an easy target.

Andrea left and drove northbound on 168th Street toward her home. She had her food next to her on the seat, and as she approached the stop sign at Fort Street, she noticed the car ahead of her was slowing to a crawl.

Within seconds Nikko Jenkins hopped from the backseat of his car, ran toward Andrea, and yanked her into the street. Moments later he shot her numerous times with a 9-millimeter rifle, leaving her for dead just south of the four-way intersection.

The *Omaha World-Herald* reported that Christine Bordeaux later cooperated with law enforcement and told a grisly tale of how the four suspects were cruising West Omaha, well after midnight, looking for a target to rob.

Erica Jenkins was driving, next to Christine Bordeaux. Nikko and his uncle Levering were in the backseat.

Bordeaux later recalled how Kruger screamed, "No, no, please don't," as Nikko Jenkins pulled her from her car.

Kruger was shot four times by Nikko Jenkins. She was struck in the head twice, and in the neck and shoulder. She died instantly at the scene.

Jenkins and Levering left in Andrea Kruger's car, following Erica Jenkins and Christine Bordeaux.

Bordeaux told law enforcement that Erica called her brother Nikko and screamed, "Why didn't you move that body into the ditch? That was stupid."

And if this situation could not be worse, or more grotesque, Warren Levering ate the food bought by Andrea Kruger in the McDonald's drive-through lane.

All four suspects were convicted of their crimes. Nikko Jenkins was sentenced to death in the State of Nebraska. The spree killer awaits his lethal injection on death row.

Is the death penalty justified here?

COLD AND CALCULATED

There are other cases of cold, calculated murders in Omaha that have caused debate about the death penalty.

Serial killer Anthony Garcia killed four people in a five-year period (2008 to 2013), including eleven-year-old Thomas Hunter, who was stabbed to death in his midtown Omaha residence after he returned home from school.

The killing of young Hunter and the housekeeper remained unsolved for years until the puzzle pieces started to fit once Garcia came back to Omaha and killed again.

Garcia's motive: Hunter's father, a medical doctor (along with another of the later victims, also a physician), gave Garcia negative evaluations while Garcia was studying at the Creighton University School of Medicine, located in Omaha.

Dr. Hunter wasn't home when Garcia came to his house with revenge on his mind. Garcia killed the son and housekeeper simply because they were in the house.

The second killings, five years later, occurred when Garcia went to the home of the second physician who gave him poor reviews as a medical student. He killed the doctor and his wife.

Anthony Garcia sits on death row in the State of Nebraska.

In November 2005 twelve-year-old Amber Harris was last seen getting off her school bus next to Kountze Park in North Omaha. Her remains were found six months later buried in Hummel Park, north of the city. She died of blunt force trauma to the head.

Roy Ellis, fifty-three and a convicted sex offender, was convicted of Amber's murder.

After he was sentenced to death, Amber's mother exclaimed, "He's earned his access to hell. My hatred for him is off the scale."

Roy Ellis is awaiting execution in Nebraska too.

THE VOTERS SPEAK

On February 8, 2008, the Nebraska Supreme Court declared in *State v. Mata* that electrocution constitutes a "cruel and unusual punishment" under the Nebraska Constitution. The state legislature subsequently approved a bill to change its method of execution to lethal injection, which was signed by Governor Dave Heineman on May 28, 2009.

Nebraska was the last state to adopt lethal injection as its execution method.

In May 2015, the Nebraska State Legislature voted 32–15 on a measure to abolish the death penalty in the state. The bill was sponsored by Senator Ernie Chambers, who had introduced similar pieces of legislation over prior decades. Governor Pete Ricketts vetoed the legislation, but the legislature voted 30–19 to override the veto.

Therefore, Nebraska had no death penalty on the books.

In summer 2015, an organization called Nebraskans for the Death Penalty gathered signatures on petitions to repeal the bill. The petition organizers submitted 120,479 valid signatures, more than 10 percent of the registered voters in the state, and thus enough to suspend the bill and preserve the death penalty until a public vote could be held.

In the November 2016 general election, the death-penalty repeal was rejected by 61 percent of the voters, thereby retaining capital punishment in the state.

Senator Chambers, a frequent critic of the criminal justice system and law enforcement, voiced his frustration in the *Omaha World-Herald* by saying that Nebraska remains a "hidebound and backward state."

"I have been in this activity too long to be surprised by what happened tonight," Senator Chambers said. "It will not dishearten me; it will not deter me."

THE WOMAN BEHIND *DEAD MAN WALKING*

During the winter of 2018 I attended a lecture at a local Catholic university geared toward the death penalty in Nebraska. I saw the advertisement in the paper for the speaker Sister Helen Prejean, a Catholic nun.

I had never heard of her before, but I noted she had written the book *Dead Man Walking*, which was subsequently made into a movie I have watched several times over the years. I'm a big Susan Sarandon fan, and when I read that her role in the movie was based on Sister Prejean, I thought it was worth braving the Nebraska cold to hear her presentation.

I expected a hundred people or so to attend. After all, how many people have heard of Sister Helen Prejean? Therefore, I was surprised to find the gym was packed, with a standing-room-only crowd. I forgot how "Catholic" Omaha, Nebraska, is.

I was correct in my assumption that I was one of the few pro–death penalty people in attendance. Judging from the signs, shirts, and questions, it was clear that Sister Prejean was facing a friendly crowd.

Sister Prejean started her lecture by pointing out that prior to the 1960s, the death penalty was viewed by many as being utilized to protect society and not to address the crime that had occurred.

I immediately thought of the execution by electric chair of Nebraskan Charles Starkweather, one of the first infamous spree killers in the United States. Starkweather, then nineteen, and his girlfriend, Caril Ann Fugate, just fourteen, terrorized Nebraska and Wyoming between December 1957 and January 1958 while murdering eleven people.

In 1959 Starkweather was electrocuted at the Nebraska State Penitentiary. I have since scanned articles about Starkweather and his murderous rampage. There was frequent mention about how citizens of Nebraska could now "sleep soundly" and not fear him anymore, now that he was dead.

Note: In February 2020 the Nebraska Board of Pardons turned down a request by Fugate, now seventy-six, for a hearing to clear her name. Released on parole in 1976, Fugate has long maintained her innocence and states she, at the age of fourteen, was an unwilling accomplice on Starkweather's reign of terror.

Sister Prejean was an engaging speaker. Quiet and unassuming, she did not hammer the crowd with liberal rants or judgments about those who support the death penalty. Instead, she emphasized the importance of forgiving those who committed such heinous acts that resulted in the imposition of the death penalty being handed down by a judge or group of judges.

I wrote a note during this portion of the lecture stating, "I say, why forgive?" She said something that I frequently hear from death penalty opponents: "The death penalty revictimizes us as a society."

My notes read, "The guy on death row is not a victim, he is a convicted felon who killed someone."

I was in total disagreement with her in one area of her talk, and I fought with my emotions not to get up and walk out. She said, "The guards in the penitentiaries kill these death row inmates."

I quickly and aggressively scrawled notes, noting that "to me, killers take a life illegally."

Correctional department employees "legally execute inmates, based on a judge's decision."

In fairness to Sister Prejean, she did note that "guards and wardens are good people," and she formed friendships with them over her many years of working in the correctional facilities.

DEATH PENALTY FOE SISTER HELEN PREJEAN TO SPEAK AT COLLEGE OF ST. MARY

By Blake Ursch / World-Herald Staff writer

Feb 4, 2018

Sister Helen Prejean is not surprised that, in 2016, most voting Nebraskans chose to reinstate the death penalty.

Referendums, she said, usually swing in favor of the "surface soul" of people. The part that says: "This was a terrible crime, and the person responsible deserves to die."

But if the average person could pull back the curtain and see an execution for what it really is, she said, it might not feel so much like justice.

"There are real inequities, real injustices, and I have to put my energies on the side of helping to change those things," she said.

Prejean (pronounced "pray-John"), a Roman Catholic nun and one of the world's leading advocates for abolishing the death penalty, will speak in Omaha Tuesday as part the College of St. Mary's annual Elden Curtiss Lecture Series. The lecture begins at 7 p.m. in the college's Lied Fitness Center.

In 1993, Prejean published "Dead Man Walking," an account of her time spent serving as a spiritual adviser to death row inmates, including Elmo Patrick Sonnier, who was eventually executed for the murders of two teenagers in Louisiana. The book, nominated for a Pulitzer Prize, was later adapted into a 1995 movie starring Susan Sarandon and Sean Penn.

Prejean began writing letters to Sonnier in the early 1980s. She never expected that the experience would radically affect her worldview and set her life on a new course, she said in a recent interview with The World-Herald.

"I call that the sneaky Jesus," she said. "Two years later, I am there with him watching him be executed in the electric chair. It changed my life, because I saw the execution of human beings for what it was: a premeditated killing."

Prejean has spent the last three decades counseling prisoners and families of murder victims, while working to educate the public about the death penalty. She has given speeches all over the world, including Omaha. In 2012, she delivered the commencement address at the College of St. Mary.

Her ministry has also brought her face-to-face with other death row inmates, including Nebraska's Harold "Willie" Otey. In 1978, Otey confessed to raping and murdering 26-year-old Jane McManus in her Pacific Street home. In 1994, he was put to death by electric chair—the state's first execution since that of Charles Starkweather 35 years before.

Prejean met with Otey before his execution at the Nebraska State Penitentiary in Lincoln. There, she said, she was struck by his cell—a room designed for condemned prisoners just before execution. The place reminded her of a college dorm room.

"There were no bars," she said. "I just said 'This is not going to be much of a killing state.' I still think that, referendum or not."

The way Prejean sees it, it's her job to help the public deal with outrage over violent crimes, while also making clear to people that the current system for capital punishment is, in her view, deeply flawed. The system often targets poor convicts, she said, while those with the means to afford stronger legal defenses get more lenient sentences.

Prejean said the death penalty is also disproportionately applied in cases where victims are white over cases where victims are people of color. According to the Washington, D.C.-based Death Penalty Information Center, cases with white victims have accounted for 75.6 percent of executions since 1976.

"Some lives are valued far more highly than others," Prejean said. "A victim has to have a certain status."

It's also important to consider the emotional toll a death sentence takes on victims' families, she said. In many cases, families are left waiting years and decades for an execution to be carried out, leaving opportunities for them to be traumatized again and again.

Prejean said she's also talked to prison officials tasked with carrying out executions who have told her they'll carry forever the weight of taking death row inmates' lives.

In making her arguments, Prejean said, it's important to stand with people in their outrage. Society will always demand justice for violent crimes. And it should.

But there's a problem, she said, in determining certain crimes to be worthy of death and others not.

"What we're running into is: What in the world is the most terrible crime, the most terrible murder?" she said. "How do you distinguish the worst murder from an ordinary murder? None of those categories hold when it comes to the life of a human being."

Reprinted with permission from the *Omaha World-Herald*.

Sister Prejean talked of alleged racial disparity of those being executed, as well as a perception of the death penalty being unfairly utilized when the victim is white as opposed to being a minority.

Note: As of 2020, of the twelve inmates on death row in Nebraska, three are white males.

Sister Helen Prejean, CSJ, who was the inspiration for actress Susan Sarandon's character in the movie Dead Man Walking, *spoke in Omaha.*

Finally, Sister Prejean pointed out how "morally wrong" it is to kill a "defenseless inmate." I wish she had expanded on this thought more, especially her reference to an inmate being defenseless.

After all, I reasoned, the inmate on death row had a defense attorney working for him. In the cases I have researched, multiple appeals have been filed, many heard by the Nebraska Supreme Court.

In most death row cases, the victims were the ones who were totally defenseless, resulting in the sentence of death being imposed, like Thomas Hunter who was killed because he was simply at home when someone who was mad at his father came calling. Or Andrea Kruger on her way home. And Amber Harris who got off the school bus and ran into a sexual predator.

I was glad I went to hear Sister Prejean talk. I found her warm, engaging, and committed to her cause. Yet I still could not agree with her on the death penalty for the monsters I have seen walk our streets.

51 PERCENT IN FAVOR OF THE DEATH PENALTY

While at Sister Prejean's presentation, I noticed an old friend in the crowd. Joe Jeanette is a career lawman, both on the local and federal level.

I was not surprised to see Jeanette there. I had seen him on television over the past few years at anti–death penalty rallies and giving interviews about why the death penalty should be abolished throughout the country.

I was always curious as to why he felt so strongly against the death penalty. After all, Jeanette was a police officer for seventeen years with the city of Bellevue, Nebraska, a suburb in the southern part of the Omaha metropolitan area.

For the past thirty years Jeanette has been the law enforcement coordinator for the United States Attorney's Office in Nebraska. He provides oversight, coordination, or assistance to programs in Nebraska dealing with violent crime, drug courts, domestic violence, substance abuse and drug treatment, and juvenile issues. In addition to these duties he monitors and assists other jurisdictions in the grant process for a variety of prevention, intervention, and enforcement activities.

In his current capacity he serves as the public information officer and training coordinator for the US Attorney. Jeanette has hosted and coordinated training for local, federal, and state officials on such topics as drugs and violent crime, child sexual abuse and enticement, financial investigations and money laundering, crime victim issues, and legal liability for law enforcement managers.

Arguably, Jeanette is known by more cops in Nebraska than any other law enforcement official, which only further piques my interest about his stance on the death penalty.

The most infamous case Jeanette was directly involved in was the 1984 arrest of John Joubert.

Joubert, an enlisted radar technician from nearby Offutt Air Force Base, was convicted for the torture and killing of two boys, ages twelve and thirteen, during separate abductions in the Bellevue area. These grizzly crimes gripped the Omaha area, and there was much relief when Joubert was finally arrested four months after the first murder. What he did to those boys was gruesome.

Joubert was executed in the Nebraska electric chair in 1996.

In 2020 Joe Jeanette agreed to sit down with me to discuss his views on the death penalty.

I respect people like Jeanette who have the guts to take a stand on an issue that puts them in direct conflict with their base of support. I admire the fact he has built up enough respect and credibility over his forty years in the arena to withstand any criticism he receives.

I first brought up the John Joubert case.

"I had a pretty good role in that," Jeanette said. "I actually sat across from him [Joubert] during breaks from his interrogations, and at one point had lunch with him."

Joubert confessed to the horrific crimes, and a city was able to sleep a little better that night knowing the monster was off the streets.

Jeanette recalled an utterance Joubert made while eating lunch: "Joubert said, 'I wonder if I'll get the death penalty.'"

"There was no doubt that the guy, in my opinion, deserved the death penalty," Jeanette said.

Joubert received the death penalty (by electrocution) in 1996 for killing two teenage boys in Nebraska in the early 1980s.

He recalls having doubts about the death penalty prior to the Joubert case, but the enormity of what was done to these boys had an impact. "And, for one thing, looking across from this guy that, you know, committed two murders ..."

But Jeanette recalls hearing a top law enforcement official being interviewed on television about Joubert and the death penalty.

"The question [from the reporter] was how much are you in favor of the death penalty? And I'll never forget his words," Jeanette said. "'Tonight, I'm 51 percent in favor of it.' And I thought, that's kind of where I am."

I asked Jeanette what some of his main concerns are about carrying out executions on death row inmates. He is right in that some smaller law enforcement jurisdictions are not as well equipped to handle homicide investigations as may be larger departments with specialized units.

This could lead to tainted confessions and improper promises being made to elicit a confession that ultimately is the driving force for a murder conviction.

An example Jeanette used was the prosecution of six individuals in Beatrice, Nebraska, which led to their convictions for the 1985 homicide of an elderly woman. Known in the media as the Beatrice 6, all six suspects were exonerated in 2009 after spending a total of seventy-five years in prison for a homicide they did not commit. Many of the convictions were based on improper interrogation tactics that elicited confessions.

DNA evidence led to the discovery of the actual suspect. In July 2016, a jury awarded the Beatrice 6 a settlement of $28 million. Gage County, Nebraska, appealed and the case reached the Supreme Court of the United States, which denied the appeal on March 4, 2019. The taxpayers of Gage County, population 21,000, are on the hook for the $28 million payment.

Jeanette stressed he is not soft toward crime. "I think if you're doing your time, that's tough."

Regarding those convicted of heinous murders he said, "Give them twenty-three and one [meaning twenty-three hours in a cell per day]. To me, that's a hell of a punishment."

He said, "So it's not like I'm swinging on the Eighth Amendment [protecting inmates from cruel and unusual punishment]. So many millions of dollars go through the appeal process. I think it would be so much easier to lock these guys up and isolate them."

Jeanette said, "Obviously, it's not a deterrent to crime. I don't think that anybody's out there going, oh man, I saw that guy get executed, I guess maybe I shouldn't commit that murder."

I agree. The death penalty is not a deterrent to crime.

Jeanette also pointed out a perceived disparate impact on minorities and inconsistency in sentencing on death penalty cases for reasons to doubt the effectiveness. He made an interesting point on how death penalty cases may not provide closure to family members of the victims.

"I talked to a young lady whose father was slain. He was a police officer in Iowa, and I asked, 'How'd you feel when the killer was sentenced to life because that's all you can get in Iowa?' And she goes, 'I was angry. But then, I don't feel that whatever happens to this guy is going to bring me any closure.'"

Jeanette's main concern with the death penalty lies with the imperfections of the criminal justice system, resulting in the possibility of the wrong person being put to death.

Joe Jeanette, veteran law enforcement officer, opposed to the death penalty.

I challenged him by pointing out that the John Joubert case provided no doubt he was guilty of torturing and viciously killing the two boys.

The conviction of Roberto C. Martinez-Marinero, who tossed his four-year-old brother into the Elkhorn River to conceal the death of their mother, cast no doubt he was guilty.

The conviction of Nikko Jenkins in multiple murders, including the senseless death of Andrea Kruger, is rock solid.

I asked, "In situations like this, does it change your mind at all as to how you view the death penalty?"

"No, it doesn't," Jeanette responded. "I'm not willing to give up on those questionable cases."

Jeanette has taken some heat from cops and coworkers but does not rule out working on causes in the future to oppose the death penalty.

ON DEATH ROW FOR THIRTY-NINE YEARS

In the summer of 1979, twenty-one-year-old Carey Dean Moore robbed and murdered two cab drivers in Omaha. He later confessed to police and was convicted in 1980 of two counts of first-degree murder. On June 20, 1980, a three-judge panel sentenced Moore to death.

Convicted killer Carey Dean Moore lived on death row for thirty-nine years before being executed for his crimes. (Photo courtesy of Nebraska Department of Corrections.)

On August 14, 2018, thirty-nine years after his murders, Moore was executed by lethal injection by the State of Nebraska. It was the first execution in Nebraska using lethal injection, and the first use of capital punishment in Nebraska since 1997. The execution was the first in the United States to use the powerful opioid fentanyl.

Numerous individuals told of Moore's remorse, growth, and maturity while in prison for those many years.

Does the fact that Moore lived on death row for thirty-nine years before being executed diminish the impact of the death penalty?

I ended the interview with Jeanette by illustrating the images I have of poor little Josue Marinero being ripped from the backseat of the car, while crying and screaming, and being tossed over the dark bridge into the river, where he endured a horrible death while drowning, with nobody there to save him.

"Joe, this is something that has been in my mind for years. I just can't wrap my head around the idea of this little boy being thrown into the river."

"I struggle with that, I do, Mark," he said. "I'll struggle with it and then look back on the bigger picture of things."

Roberto C. Martinez-Marinero did not receive the death penalty for this crime. He has the rest of his life to ponder his little brother's last thoughts, while dirty river water was filling his lungs.

I understand Jeanette's concerns about racial disparity, monies spent on appeals, and potentially executing the wrong individual.

But do Martinez-Marinero or Jenkins or Garcia or Joubert deserve to have the needle stuck into their arm for the fatal dose to be delivered? My answer is yes.

Some crimes are so heinous and cruel that the proper punishment is to execute the perpetrators.

My struggle with the death penalty continues.

20

JOE COOL LIVES UP TO HIS NAME

One of the best perks of being a police officer is the ability to be near famous people. Whether it's Los Angeles, New York, or Omaha, security is needed whenever politicians, movie stars, or athletes come to town. I frequently volunteered for security details because I loved the excitement associated with guarding the rich and famous.

In the early 1980s President Ronald Reagan came to the Omaha Civic Auditorium for an event. I was assigned as a uniformed officer to stand on the corner of 19th and Capitol Avenue downtown to monitor the crowd.

The US Secret Service held a thorough briefing prior to the president's arrival. I was in awe of the formalized planning it took just to transport President Reagan the few miles from the Omaha airport to the venue site.

I recall the agent in charge talking of the possibility of protesters lying on the street in front of the moving presidential limousine. "If that occurs," he said, "the limo will not stop. We will run over any protester and keep the motorcade moving."

I remember thinking I wanted to see that.

We were also told that under no circumstances should we as uniformed police officers turn and look at the presidential limousine as it passed by us on the way back to the airport. Our sole focus was on the crowd that was waving and yelling as the motorcade passed by us. The Secret Service made that abundantly clear.

But I also wondered about how many chances I would ever have to look at a president as he passes within ten feet of me. So I admit that as President Reagan passed by me on my post, I turned and nodded at him, and I swear he waved back at me.

Or maybe he was acknowledging the thousands of people I was separating from him.

I was also on the security detail for Vice President George H. W. Bush as he held a luncheon at Peony Park (a meeting venue in an amusement park) in midtown Omaha. He and his wife, Barbara, passed within feet of me, and I recall thinking of how genuinely nice and pleasant they both seemed.

In the spring of 1995 Joe Montana came to Omaha as a spokesman for Hanes underwear. Omaha was opening one of the first Super Targets in the northwest part of the city, and Montana was the featured celebrity. Thousands of fans were expected to line up for a picture with Joe along with a signed autograph.

Joe Montana was winding down his fabulous football career. He was thirty-eight years old at the time, and his path to the Pro Football Hall of Fame was a certainty. Selected in the third round of the 1979 draft as the 82nd player, Montana had already won four Super Bowls with the San Francisco 49ers. In three of those Super Bowls he was selected as the most valuable player. Montana's all-time passer rating still ranks as one of the highest ever.

Besides all this, Montana also won a national championship at the University of Notre Dame.

Montana's nickname was Joe Cool, a testament to the leadership and calmness he displayed during his entire career.

When I was asked to help guard Montana on that sunny weekend afternoon, I jumped at the chance. I was a huge fan and wasn't going to pass up this opportunity. I would be wearing my formal police uniform and wanted Joe Montana to have the impression that I was all business when it came to protecting him during his visit to Omaha.

The event started at 1:00 p.m., and Joe arrived at the Target store via limo about an hour before. We hustled him into a side door away from the view of the throngs of fans that were lined up for blocks waiting to meet him. We took him into the back storage area of the store where we could simply lead him directly out a nondescript door onto the stage when the event started.

For an hour it was me, another officer, and Joe Montana. I tried my best to keep my professional demeanor about me and not let on how excited I was to be with him. Joe was so easy to talk to and asked us about our careers as police officers. For close to a half hour we regaled him with our best war stories, and he kept asking for more.

He genuinely seemed excited by what he was hearing and told us he would have enjoyed being a police officer. Once Joe said that, I saw my opening, and I took it. I said, "Joe, I think you made a better decision becoming an NFL quarterback!"

We all laughed, and I began asking him about his career. I was respectful not to ask if he was retiring, as was being reported on such networks as ESPN. But I recall asking him how he felt winning Super Bowls, setting records, and throwing the winning touchdown pass to Dwight Clark in the 1981 NFC championship game against the Dallas Cowboys. Years later the Montana-to-Clark connection is still known as "The Catch."

Montana was humble, engaging, and willing to talk to us. It's a time in my life I'll never forget.

He was wearing a long-sleeved blue turtleneck sweater and blue jeans, and I remember thinking how skinny he looked.

"Joe," I said, "don't take this wrong, but you don't look like the best quarterback to ever play the game."

He laughed heartily at that one and said he had heard it before.

We were about fifteen minutes from show time, and I asked Joe if he would sign a football for me. Without hesitation he said yes, but I had several problems to deal with first. I had no football with me, and I couldn't leave Joe to go buy one.

A stock boy happened to be walking close to us, and I yelled, "Hey, can you stop for a second?" I think he was scared to death when being told to stop by a uniformed police officer, but I quickly alleviated his fear.

"Would you do me a favor?" I asked. "Here's forty bucks. Go buy me a football as quick as you can, and I'll let you keep the change."

The kid ran off and within minutes came back into the warehouse huffing and out of breath. He had a brand-new football still in the box that he proudly handed me, and I thanked him profusely. We had about five minutes before Joe made his appearance, so I tore the ball from the box and handed it to Joe Cool.

After several seconds, to my horror, Montana exclaimed, "I'm not signing this football!" My heart stopped momentarily, and I remember asking myself what I could possibly have done to piss him off.

"Why not, Joe?" I asked in a low tone of voice.

In one hand he palmed the ball and shoved the front of it toward my face. "It's a Dan Marino football!" he yelled, trying to keep a straight face.

Joe did sign the ball, and he was a great guy to deal with the entire day. He signed thousands of autographs for adoring fans, and, finally, at the end of the day, it was time for other officers to take him back to the airport.

As his limo drove off, I was walking to my car when my police portable radio crackled: "Joe to Mark, Joe to Mark."

Obviously, one of the officers with him in the limo had handed his microphone to Montana.

"Go ahead, Joe," I responded, not quite believing what I was hearing.

"It was nice meeting you and thanks for everything."

"Good luck to you, Joe, and congratulations on a great career," I said, knowing I would relish this moment forever. Joe Cool lived up to his nickname.

Montana retired several months later and never played football again.

Protecting Joe Montana during his 1995 promotional appearance in Omaha.

PART II
FROM BUSTING METH LABS
TO CHASING BLACK LABS

21

JAKE THE PUPPY
(NOT A HAPPY DOG STORY)

I left the Omaha Police Department after twenty-six years to take a position as Vice President of Field Operations for the Nebraska Humane Society. It was said that I left the job of busting meth labs to chasing black Labs.

Humor aside, I made animal cruelty a priority.

For fifteen years in that second act of my law enforcement career, I came across hundreds of cases of animal abuse being connected with domestic violence.

Domestic violence and animals are a bad mix. People who hurt animals don't stop with animals. It is critically important that cruelty toward animals be taken seriously by law enforcement, and by society at large. This is not just for the sake of the animals themselves.

Ample research backs up the finding that there is a direct link between acts of cruelty to animals and violence toward humans, which includes child abuse, domestic violence, elder abuse, and other violent behavior.

Animal abusers are in fact five times more likely to also harm other humans, according to a landmark 1997 study by the Massachusetts Society for the Prevention of Cruelty to Animals and Northeastern University. Another study, published in 2013, found that 43 percent of those who commit school massacres also committed acts of cruelty to animals—generally against cats and dogs.

Animal abuse was found in 88 percent of homes in which physical adult or child abuse was being investigated, said one study. And research shows that if a child is cruel to animals, it may be a sign that serious abuse or neglect has been inflicted on the child. Children who witness animal abuse are at greater risk of becoming abusers themselves.

A 2017 study showed that 89 percent of women who had companion animals during an abusive relationship reported that their animals were threatened, harmed, or killed by their abusive partner.

This finding is in line with other research showing that domestic violence toward pets correlates with domestic violence toward humans and is also a tool of domestic abuse—violent members of the household will threaten to hurt or actually hurt a companion animal as a method of control and a form of emotional violence.

Indeed, more than half of women in domestic violence shelters report that they delayed their escape out of fear for their animals.

The Nebraska Humane Society provides temporary and safe housing for the companion animals of domestic violence victims. Known as Project Pet Safe, NHS recognizes that many victims are reluctant to leave abusive relationships for fear of injury or death happening to their loving pets. By joining with social agencies such as the Women's Center for Advancement and Catholic Charities, the Nebraska Humane Society is an active partner in the fight against domestic violence. Check into similar programs where you live.

Both because animals themselves need protection, and because of the link between cruelty to animals and cruelty to humans, violence against animals must be taken seriously under the law.

There are some ways in which the law is reflecting this seriousness. For example, all fifty states now have felony animal cruelty laws on the books. Nearly two-thirds of states allow pets to be included in domestic violence protective orders.

WHAT HAPPENS IN THE BEDROOM ...

Early in my career at the Nebraska Humane Society, we dealt with a guy named Anthony Schepis. He was the poster child for demonstrating the correlation between domestic violence and animal cruelty.

Schepis had recently bought a German Shepherd puppy he named Jake.

Jake was a beautiful dog. His soft coat of fur was brown and black in color, and his big ears and large paws made it obvious there was a lot of growth left in his future. I am sure Jake acted like most puppies. He craved attention, was high maintenance at times, and, most importantly, longed for safety and security being provided by his master.

Schepis failed miserably.

In the summer of 2006 Schepis was at home in West Omaha with his girlfriend. All indications are the relationship was contentious and volatile at times, and that Schepis had a hair-trigger temper.

Schepis lived with a male roommate who stayed in another bedroom. The roommate was awakened after midnight by the arguing and screaming between Schepis and the girlfriend, while in Schepis's next-door bedroom.

In later interviews the roomie told me this was not an uncommon occurrence. According to him, Schepis and his girlfriend were frequently heard slapping and hitting each other. Instead of calling the police department, the roomie simply rolled over and went back to sleep.

Police departments across the country handle domestic violence calls much differently than how I was trained over forty years ago. I was able to find my notes from October 20, 1978, about a class taught to my Omaha Police Department recruit class titled "Domestic Complaints."

I was shocked to see that the only information I recorded were the phone numbers for the Crisis Line and Shelter for Abused Women. As a rookie police officer, I rarely made an arrest for a domestic violence situation, even if we had physical evidence of an assault. Instead, the common tactic used by cops on the street was to separate the two people by offering one a ride to another location.

Then I would verbally transmit the obligatory warning: "Now, if we come back here tonight, one of you is going to jail!" Finally, I would hit back in on the radio by telling the dispatcher "District 104, 10-8 code 6," meaning I was back in service after handling a civil matter.

Most departments now have a mandatory arrest requirement when the investigating officers see any signs of physical abuse on either of the two participants. The victim of the domestic violence is not allowed to have the choice of pressing charges against the aggressor. Domestic violence calls are handled more professionally now and better ensure the safety of the victims.

A short while later he again woke up to the screaming of Anthony Schepis. This time the roommate heard only the yelling of Anthony Schepis, and not the woman.

Now, Schepis was yelling at his defenseless puppy, Jake, who could be heard whining and screaming out in pain. The roommate said that Schepis was in a fit of rage, screaming profanities at the dog. Thudding noises could be heard emanating from the room while the dog, obviously in distress, continued its guttural cries for help.

Then the room became silent.

The roommate, a lover of Jake the puppy, became concerned and knocked on the bedroom door. After entering, the roomie saw a frightening sight. Schepis has blood on his hands and tank top. There was blood on the floor, all four walls, and the ceiling.

And lying on the bed was the corpse of Jake.

The puppy had blood around his head and face, but otherwise looked like a puppy taking a nap while sprawled on its left side.

According to the roommate Schepis was shaking and incoherent. Bottles of alcohol were strewn throughout his bedroom. The roommate was shocked and decided to call 911.

Omaha Police and an investigator with the Nebraska Humane Society arrived and were met by the ghastly sight.

Law enforcement officers develop a callousness about them over the years when dealing with homicides, assaults, and victims of car accidents. But I can talk from experience how the sight of a dead puppy, beaten to death by its master in a fit of rage, can spark sadness and even tears by investigating officers. Similar responses are often felt in crimes against children.

The investigating officers treated Schepis's bedroom like a crime scene. Photographs were taken, blood splatter analysis was done, and a detailed description of the crime scene was documented.

Schepis began yelling and pleading with the officers at the scene, claiming that Jake had just been struck by a car in front of his house and that he had taken the injured puppy into his bedroom and attempted to revive the dog with chest compressions.

When confronted with his roommate's accusations, Schepis, ever the manipulator, said that his roomie had it in for him and was lying to police about what he had heard and seen.

Anthony Schepis

Omaha Police Department booking photo of Anthony Schepis, July 2006.
He was later convicted for animal abuse.

A later interview with the girlfriend confirmed that she and Schepis had been engaged in a horrible verbal and physical altercation prior to her storming out of his bedroom and leaving his house. A bully of a guy, Schepis was 5 foot 9 and weighed about 225, so he had some weight behind his ferocious punches.

Schepis then took his rage out on the remaining victim, one who could not defend himself nor escape the bedroom.

That was Jake the puppy.

Schepis was charged with felony animal cruelty and housed at the Douglas County Correctional Center in downtown

Omaha. His visitor log showed one person who continually came to visit him during his time while awaiting trial—the girlfriend.

It seems like the media love to cover crimes connected to animal cruelty. The reporters know the emotional impact these crimes have on those who watch and read about them.

I was quoted in the media as saying, "This is a severe beating of this dog. The Nebraska Humane Society works closely with domestic violence groups. Anger issues like this taken out on a defenseless puppy could easily be taken out on a child or an adult by this person."

"We're alleging that it's a felony abuse to an animal," said veteran Douglas County prosecutor Tom McKenney to the media. McKenney, a lover of German Shepherds himself, was my go-to prosecutor for animal cruelty cases. He was a true professional and an even better friend.

A Nebraska Humane Society veterinarian testified at Schepis's preliminary hearing that Jake's ribs were broken in many places. Jake also had a ruptured lung, a broken leg, and fractures to the skull. She testified that based on her experiences Jake's injuries were not consistent with being struck by a car. Rather, she confirmed that blunt force trauma, most likely with a fist, caused poor Jake's demise.

Schepis ultimately pleaded guilty to a felony charge of animal cruelty. The evidence was too overwhelming for him to refute.

A Douglas County District Judge sentenced Schepis to one to two years of free room and board with the Nebraska Department of Correctional Services. I thought the sentence was light, which was not uncommon in animal cruelty.

I always the felt the stigma of "it's just a dog" being prevalent among those in the criminal justice system.

On January 17, 2007, Anthony Schepis was found dead in his cell. Though only thirty-nine years old, Schepis suffered some type of medical emergency and could not be revived by responding emergency personnel.

Upon hearing the news, some of my coworkers and friends made it clear they had no sympathy for his demise, given the horrendous treatment of Jake the puppy during one his fits of rage.

Speaking for myself, I do not wish death on anybody. Life is precious, and who am I to gloat when a piece of shit like Anthony Schepis dies in a cramped and sweaty prison cell. And I'm certainly not qualified to say if Schepis took a direct descent to hell for his crime. That is not my decision to make.

But I take comfort in knowing that St. Francis of Assisi, the patron saint of animals, most likely had some tough questions for Schepis before determining if the up or down button on the elevator would be pushed.

In 2014 Pope Francis shocked the Catholic world by telling a young boy whose dog had just died, "One day, we will see our animals again in the eternity of Christ. Paradise is open to all God's creatures."

If that's the case, Jake the puppy is doing just fine.

22

THE TRENCH COAT (A HAPPY DOG STORY)

Sarge the dog was living the life of Riley. Black Labradors need space to exercise, and Sarge certainly had access to plenty of freedom while living on an acreage in the Platte River valley near Louisville, Nebraska.

Sarge had free range to roam through field after field, and his extra sensitive snout usually directed him back to his house where loving owners, a warm bed, and plenty of food awaited him.

Labs, besides being great companion dogs, are best known for their keen sense of smell. Labs are frequently found working in law enforcement jobs from arson and drug and bomb detection to search and rescue situations.

Sometimes the overpowering scent of rabbits, foxes, and coyotes can totally captivate dogs like good old Sarge, taking them to unfamiliar spots where they would rather not be. This happened to Sarge in the winter of 2008 when he was found stranded on an ice jam in the middle of the icy-cold Platte River, miles from home.

Sarge was spotted by a resident who lived on the river. The weather could not have been worse. It was snowing, windy, and bitter cold.

Sarge had worked his way into a colossal mess. He was surrounded by a strong river current, with the small chunk of ice he was standing on acting as his only means of survival. The Good Samaritan called the local sheriff's department, the Nebraska Humane Society, and a local television station (maybe not in that order) to try to rally help for Sarge, who was freezing while standing in the strong north wind with snow pelting his coat.

That day, I was on my way back from Lincoln, and a meeting at the Nebraska State Capitol building, when I received the call. I had spent the morning at the state legislature lobbying for an animal cruelty law that would make it a felony crime to abandon animals. Laws like this seem like a no-brainer to the average citizen, but in a rural state like Nebraska, there is frequent skepticism among the senators who represent farmers and ranchers of any proposed animal cruelty law that might impact hog, cattle, and chicken production.

I was weary driving the sixty miles back to Omaha after a long morning of convincing skeptical senators that this proposed law was the right thing to do.

I was wearing a suit, wing-tip shoes, and a tan trench coat with no lining. My wife, Annette, had told me for years to dump this archaic piece of outerwear, which was last in style when Peter Falk portrayed the TV detective Columbo in the 1970s.

But true to form I didn't listen as well as I should have. I would regret this in a matter of minutes after I arrived at the Platte River.

I met some of my animal control officers who were on scene with a sheriff's deputy and a TV crew. From the highway we couldn't see the dog due to the low visibility caused by the heavy snow and high winds.

We had to walk over a quarter mile on the frozen riverbank to get to where Sarge was stuck. This was the coldest walk I ever experienced. The trench coat provided no insulation from the frigid weather. My shoes kept falling through the ice, making my feet numb. Why did I not listen to my wife and buy a heavy-duty winter coat?

Oh, well, I figured she'll never find out. So what does it matter?

Little did I know that in less than twenty-four hours my trench coat would be front and center on NBC's *Today* show for millions to see.

We finally reached the spot on the riverbank where we could see poor Sarge. He was about fifty feet away from us, with a strong river current separating him from the shore and where he stood on an unmoving ice jam. I remember wondering how in the heck did he end up on this ice jam in the middle of the Platte River. The only answer we ever came up with is he must have fallen in the river and was able to swim to the ice block and hoist himself to safety.

Sarge the black Lab stuck on the ice jam in the Platte River.
(Taken by private photographer at the scene.)

It was obvious this would not be an easy rescue. The river was dangerous for the rescue team to navigate. We could not risk putting a safety harness on an officer and having them traverse the icy water to the dog. The only option was putting a boat in the water, which would take time. The rescue relied on Sarge's cooperation to stay put on the ice jam until help arrived.

Some of the rescue team left to get the boat. It would be over an hour before they returned, so I decided to stay and keep Sarge company. I had already lost feeling in my toes, I had no stocking cap, and my dreaded trench coat was like wearing a thin piece of Saran Wrap in the bitter cold wind.

I couldn't bring myself to leave Sarge alone. He was a handsome dog with an alert look and a mischievous doggy smile. Occasionally, he would sit down and look at me as if to ask, "What should I do here?" It was obvious to me that Sarge liked having company, even though we were separated by a swift current of freezing water.

His tail was constantly wagging, and frequently he would tip one paw in the water as if to test the temperature before potentially jumping in.

As the minutes wore on, Sarge was losing his patience. Several times he started jumping in the frigid water, causing me to frantically yell "stay, stay!"

The last thing I wanted Sarge to do was jump in that swift current. I didn't think he could survive since the current would probably drive him away from me, most certainly causing him to drown.

Finally, Sarge had enough. I could tell by the look in his eyes, and his determined body posture, that he was sick and tired of being marooned on that ice jam. I told those with me to be ready in case Sarge worked up the nerve to take the dive.

I was also cognizant of the television crew filming my every move. This would be a terrible situation if I failed to rescue this poor dog, made worse by the story being on the evening news.

Suddenly Sarge plunged into the river and immediately disappeared underwater for a few agonizing seconds. I saw him pop up about ten feet down river from where we were standing, given the strength of the current he was fighting against. I began running along the riverbank screaming for him to come to me. We all started falling on the ice since the traction was terrible (especially with my wing-tips).

I will never forget the look of determination on Sarge's face, fighting as hard as he could against the wicked current while never taking his eyes off me as I ran alongside him on the riverbank. Seconds seemed like minutes as Sarge frantically doggie paddled as hard as he could to reach safety.

As he got closer to me, I began realizing that I could easily fall into this river, in my dress suit and trench coat. The thought popped in my head that I could drown trying to save this dog. But things were happening so quickly now that I just kept running along the bank, pleading with this dog to keep coming to me.

Finally, I leaned as far as I could into the water and grabbed Sarge's scruff, that loose layer of skin directly behind a dog's ear. I pulled as hard as I could, while leaning directly over the river current, and yanked this wet and cold dog onto the riverbank. Others tended to Sarge while I took a deep breath and thought to myself, what the hell was I thinking?

I'm leading Sarge the dog to safety after his river rescue.
(Taken by private photographer at the scene.)

Sarge was happy, relieved, and appreciative. We tried to dry him off as best we could, but it was still snowing and blowing. I was able to walk Sarge on a leash the quarter mile back to our warm animal control truck, where he was whisked away to the Nebraska Humane Society for a medical exam and nice warm blankets.

Secretly, I was hoping the dog's owners would not come forward. Maybe I would be able to adopt Sarge and take care of him for the rest of his life. After all, the dog and I had just been through a harrowing experience and a bond was formed. But after seeing the story on the evening news, the owners did come to the animal shelter. They were nice people who loved their dog and were worried sick when Sarge failed to return home from an adventure.

The next morning my phone rang. My daughter, Katie, said, "Why didn't you tell me my dad was going to be on the *Today* show?"

It seems the local NBC affiliate sent the video of Sarge's rescue to the network, causing Matt Lauer to ask, "Why did the guy in the trench coat end up being the one who pulled the dog out of the water?"

And that's when Annette saw me on national TV in that awful trench coat. Forever enshrined.

Video of Sarge's rescue can be seen on YouTube at https://www.youtube.com/watch?v=_ONU28HnWUg or search **Nebraska Humane Society dog rescue Platte River.**

23

BLOOD SPORT: THE DARK SIDE OF CRIME YOU'VE NEVER SEEN

This chapter is not for the faint of heart.

When I retired from the Omaha Police Department in late 2004, I left with the notion that I had already seen everything life had to offer, and nothing in the world could surprise me. After all, I witnessed people dying in front of me, kids subjected to horrendous acts, and the overall extent of humans interacting with each other to reach their full potential of evil.

In my career at the Nebraska Humane Society, I realized I would be dealing with a new type of evil. These gritty and gut-wrenching cases I investigated during my almost fifteen years as Vice President of Field Operations at the Nebraska Humane Society (NHS) are not pretty, and there is little humor in telling these stories.

But it is important to know these crimes exist; they are important to prosecute; and they have an adverse effect on the society we live in.

My role at NHS was to supervise a staff that was dedicated to the prosecution of animal cruelty crimes. Though we had limited law enforcement authority, we worked hand-in-hand with local police departments on animal neglect and cruelty crimes, including cases involving hoarding animals in unlivable conditions and beating and starving dogs to death.

We dealt with abandoned herds of cattle, hogs, and horses left to starve. One case in particular that doesn't leave my mind are the horses we found, near death, eating bark off nearby trees as a form of nourishment (I'm happy to report our staff successfully saved and rehabilitated these fine animals).

I am on the record stating that human abuse is worse than animal cruelty. Many times, in my second career at NHS, I was questioned by citizens, defense attorneys, and the media about my views on animal cruelty and how it stacks up against the horrendous scenarios that humans endure on a daily basis. I never wavered in my answer: Abusing kids is worse than torturing a dog.

But I learned early on in my career at the Nebraska Humane Society how the act of animal cruelty transcends so many other types of crimes. Rarely did we investigate an animal cruelty case that didn't involve drugs or alcohol abuse. Rarely did we investigate a dogfighting ring that was not fraught with dangerous gang activity.

I also realized early on in my animal-saving career how important it was to have contacts in the law enforcement and prosecutorial world. In order to maintain those contacts, I knew how vital it was to portray the Nebraska Humane Society's Field Operations Department not as a tree-hugging, left-wing animal rights organization but as a professional quasi-law enforcement agency with well-trained and dedicated professionals who knew what they were doing, both inside and outside of the courtroom.

I am a big fan of author John Maxwell and his many books dedicated to achieving the ultimate in leadership abilities. In *The 21 Irrefutable Laws of Leadership*, Maxwell talks about leadership principle number 2, The Law of Influence. Basically, Maxwell writes that the more positive influence a leader can exert on both internal and external entities, the higher his or her chances are of achieving their goals.

Maxwell says, "The true measure of leadership is influence—nothing more, nothing less."

So in my career at the Nebraska Humane Society I did my best to exert positive influence with coworkers, police officers, law enforcement officials, prosecutors, public defenders, private defense attorneys, other animal control agencies, and media outlets to better ensure I would get what I wanted: the prosecution and incarceration of those involved in horrendous acts against animals.

I did hundreds of media stories during my career with NHS. The media is fascinated with animal cruelty stories. Sadly, the gorier the better. But I also realized the media raised the awareness of animal cruelty in the community. I frequently have people approach me in public places talking about how appalled they were with a particular story.

There were haters out there, those who thought I was putting the lives of animals above those of human beings. As I've previously said, this was not my intention. But it was not my job to investigate crimes against humans anymore. It was my job to go after those who preyed on the four-legged victims with no voice, who had no way to defend themselves.

I took this role seriously and used the law of influence to get this done.

Here are some of those stories.

COCK-A-DOODLE-DOO

On Labor Day in 2017, around 5:00 p.m., I received one of the strangest text messages ever.

The Field Director for the Nebraska Humane Society, who reported directly to me, texted: *We have a dick-fighting house. Need to do a warrant now. OPD holding the scene.*

I did a double-take, realizing a reference to "dick-fighting" may have applied more to my previous days in the Omaha Police Department's vice squad. Several seconds later a new text came in: *OMG-cockfighting house. Damn Auto Correct!*

As the Field Director, Kelli Brown was the supervisor for the animal control officers of the Nebraska Humane Society. The officers respond to over 30,000 calls yearly in the Omaha area, so Kelli kept quite busy putting out fires and handling day-to-day operations.

But Kelli was also a tenacious investigator who went above and beyond in the higher-level animal cruelty investigations we handled. She lived and breathed the job and was totally dedicated to do the best investigation possible to obtain convictions in court for animal abusers.

I frequently bragged to police officers of Kelli's search warrant–writing skills, which I knew were top-notch based on writing hundreds of warrants myself for drug dealers while at the Omaha Police Department.

So if Kelli Brown told me we needed to jump on this cockfighting case, I knew it to be true.

COCKFIGHTING

Cockfighting is a crime in which roosters are placed in a ring and forced to fight to the death for the amusement of onlookers. Cockfighting is illegal throughout the United States and is a felony crime in most states, including Nebraska.

Roosters are born, raised, and trained to fight on game farms. Breeders kill the birds they deem inferior, keeping only the birds who are the most game—meaning willing to fight. Breeders condition the birds to fight through physical work, including running long obstacle courses or on treadmills and through practice fights with other birds.

Breeders often pluck the birds' feathers and hack off the roosters' wattles and/or combs (the flesh at the top of their heads and under their beaks) to prevent other roosters from tearing them off in the ring. Some breeders cut off the birds' spurs, which are the natural bony protrusions on the legs, so that more deadly, artificial weapons can be strapped to their legs. In organized cock-fights, the roosters' natural fighting instincts are exaggerated by using steroids and vitamins.

Cockfights are usually held in round or square enclosures called cockpits or simply pits. With neck feathers fanned and wings whirring, the birds jump and parry at each other. They kick and duel in midair, striking at each other with razors tied to their feet and with their beaks.

Gambling is the main motivation for cockfighting. Law enforcement is aware that cockfighting transcends other crimes like drug dealing and illegal weapon possession. Organizers are weary of law enforcement and frequently change the location of the cockfights.

Normally, the fight does not end until one rooster is dead or nearly dead. Losing birds are often discarded in a barrel or trash can near the game pit, even if they're still alive.

I arrived about twenty minutes after the text to a sea of police cruisers and Nebraska Humane Society vehicles. The media were already on the scene across the street after hearing the call come out over the police scanner. The house was located along a busy four-lane street, less than a mile south of Interstate 80, which runs through the heart of Omaha.

The small, tan one-story house sat on a neat quarter-acre of land with a large detached garage. The house was well kept and had that beautiful smell of Mexican dishes having been prepared there recently.

The suspect, Jose, was handcuffed in the living room. His wife was in the driveway talking to officers.

I requested a briefing from the on-scene Omaha Police command officer.

They were dispatched for a domestic disturbance involving a husband and his wife. It seems like things may have gotten out of hand, and Jose, a short squatty guy with thick black hair and mustache, appeared intoxicated.

Many times, on calls like this, wives will scream things that normally would not come out of their mouths. In those few moments they want to see their husbands suffer at the hands of the police for what they have done to her—whatever that may be.

Note: *My best informants over the years have been scorned women. In fact, some of the best drug-dealing arrests I made during my career on the Omaha Police Department were based on information supplied by wives or girlfriends who, for whatever reason, were so furious at their significant other that all they wanted was him rotting in prison. Later most regretted giving the information, but by that time it was too late. I'm not sure what prompted Jose's wife to rat him out, but I'm sure he regrets doing what he did. My advice to criminals is this: Don't piss off your woman!*

So, when this wife began yelling that her husband, Jose, was a cockfighter and had evidence of this in the garage, the police became interested. Jose did not help his cause when, while in custody of the police inside his house, he tried to run to another room to hide his keys. In fact, the police had to taser Jose since he was acting so aggressively.

The wife also indicated that Jose had taken some of his birds to a cockfight the night before, though she did not know where.

Jose did not want us to get into that garage, which made us even more curious.

Kelli obtained a search warrant, and upon opening the garage door, we found what we suspected.

Twenty hens and roosters were confined in ten hutch cages. The garage was neat, the cages clean, and the birds had food and water. It was obvious great care had been taken to build these hutches. There was a white fan on the floor providing air circulation. However, the temperature in the garage was a balmy 93 degrees when we opened it, which was way too hot for the two dogs we also located. The German Shepherd and the boxer mix were panting heavily.

Many of the birds had their combs and wattles removed, most likely not by a trained veterinarian. We located one aggressive rooster who had injuries consistent with recent cockfighting. The bird had round punctures all over the chest and legs and inside the wings. These punctures had purple solution applied to them. A bottle of Gentian Violet, a purple antiseptic dye used to treat infections of the skin, was found in the garage.

The wounds on this bird smelled horribly based on the infection that had set in. This bird was extremely aggressive toward the other birds and to the Nebraska Humane Society personnel on the scene.

Other birds had injuries matching recent cockfighting matches. Also located during the search were hormone supplement powders, both new and used syringes, and shipping boxes showing that poultry had been shipped from locations as far as Texas and California.

Photographs were found in the house showing birds in cages and of a cockfight taking place on the ground at an unknown location.

Jose was arrested and booked on a felony cockfighting charge. We had long suspected there was a well-connected cock-fighting organization in the Omaha area, and Jose seemed to be but one part of this operation.

We were determined to find the others.

COCK PARTY

Marvin Vogler was well known by both the Cass County, Nebraska, sheriff's office and the county board. Vogler, in his late sixties, lived a few miles south of Louisville along busy Highway 50, and twenty miles south of Omaha. He took care of his aged mother in a small ranch-style house that overlooked a vast spread of barns and outbuildings.

Vogler tended to rent out his buildings for large parties. This drew the ire of county officials since his property was not zoned for such activity. In fact, Vogler had converted a two-story older barn into a party haven, complete with couches, chairs, televisions, gaming tables, and lots of nooks and crannies for partiers to hide for various nefarious activities.

In 2014 one such event drew a crowd of dangerous Omaha gang members and resulted in shots being fired and a partygoer being wounded. This was not a common occurrence for rural Cass County, and Vogler was warned by the county board not to allow such an event to occur again.

So in late November 2018, when a tipster came to the Nebraska Humane Society to tell of a large cockfighting event taking place later that day at a property south of Louisville, the sheriff's staff knew right away the informant was talking about Marvin Vogler and his property of ill repute.

At 12:30 p.m. several deputies arrived, not prepared for what they were to encounter. As they turned off Highway 50, heading down a hill toward the barns and sheds on Vogler's property, they spotted over forty cars and trucks parked on either side of the gravel drive.

It appeared most of the activity was not at the two-story party barn, but instead at a smaller one-story structure on the east end of the property. The deputies parked as close as they could, given the multitude of the vehicles present, and began walking toward the location of activity.

As soon as one person spotted the uniformed officers, all hell broke loose. Men, women, and children burst from the west door of the building, running to the north and east toward a creek and cornfield on the other side of the property. Some of the men broke out windows along the east wall, leaving blood stains where they cut themselves.

For several minutes it was total chaos, with the deputies trying their best to contain the situation before everybody was able to scatter into the fields.

I arrived as quickly as I could, along with Field Director Kelli Brown, a staff veterinarian from the Nebraska Humane Society, and several of our animal control officers. When I pulled down the gravel road, the scene had calmed down. I noticed a row of suspects, all sitting on the ground by sheriff's cruisers. There were probably twenty, mostly Hispanic, though there was a Caucasian man sitting in the group. Sadly, there was a child among the adults, probably ten years old, with a scared look on his face.

As soon as I arrived, I was briefed that additional sheriff's deputies and Nebraska state troopers were still rounding up suspects who fled from the barn. I watched as suspect after suspect was walked back in handcuffs or transported on ATVs. Drones were put into the air, with one finding a group of three to four suspects lying in a ravine looking up at the device and knowing their escape was short-lived.

The barn consisted of sheet metal walls and concrete blocks. The old gray roof was missing some shingles, adding credibility to the age of the structure. Outside there was junk everywhere consisting of stacks of wood pallets, old chairs, and a boat on a red trailer covered by a gray tarp.

The deputies did a protective sweep of the barn to verify nobody who could harm us was hiding. During the sweep they saw live birds, money, and a fighting ring. It was apparent we had stumbled onto a large-scale cockfighting operation. The on-scene commander of the Cass County sheriff's department ordered that a search warrant be obtained.

Luckily, the temperatures were decent. The arrests, totaling over thirty and still at the scene, were comfortable but saying little. Most claimed not to speak English, which made it more difficult to determine their identities.

The sun had set, it was getting dark, and we knew an ice storm would soon descend upon us. Portable lighting for both inside and outside was brought in. I wanted to get things done soon.

Cockfighting ring located in Cass County barn in 2018.

Several hours later the deputy arrived with the search warrant, and the search began. We were horrified upon entering the barn.

The first thing I saw were dead birds in the trash can, bloodied and mutilated. It was obvious to me they were fresh and had just been killed that afternoon. I knew this was going to be a rough night.

Next to the trash cans with dead birds was the fighting pen. It was built with four-foot-high sheet metal secured by wooden posts. The twenty-foot by twenty-foot ring was larger than I thought it would be, and I could see bloodstains in the dirt floor and on the sheet metal. My mind went to the small child outside who was with the suspects and who was forced to watch these birds slash each other to the death.

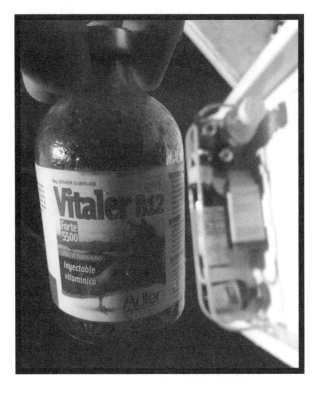

Vitamin supplement located in Cass County barn during raid.

Scads of cockfighting paraphernalia were found all around the fighting ring. Money and cell phones had been thrown to the ground. Handwritten records denoting first names of men, the bird's name, and won and loss records were located.

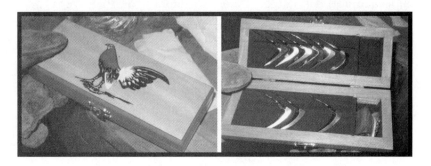

A beautifully decorated wooden box found at the raid. It contained razor-sharp spurs to attach to the birds' feet.

An old, dirty refrigerator sat along the north wall. In it were bottles of vitamin supplements most likely injected into the birds to improve their fighting prowess. Bottles of Catosal B12 and Ivomec were accompanied by syringes.

By far the most interesting evidence we found were several beautifully monogrammed wooden boxes containing stunningly designed razor-sharp spurs, used to attach to the birds' feet in order to incapacitate and kill their opponents. These boxes of spurs were lovingly maintained and most likely handed down from generation to generation. Some of the spurs were encased in diamond-studded sheaths.

We seized 186 birds from Martin Vogler's property that night. Some were found in the barn, but most were confined in over 100 makeshift cages to the north of the barn. It was cold, getting colder, and we just kept finding more birds.

I talked to Vogler that night, and he denied any knowledge of the 186 birds on his property, what they were being used for, or the cockfighting event in his barn that afternoon. He was nowhere near his property when the raid occurred, so he was not charged.

Birds seized from 2018 Cass County raid were held at the Nebraska Humane Society for disposition.

But in my forty-year law enforcement career I often cited the "plausible deniability" claim when I interviewed guilty people. The ability of some to deny knowledge of (or responsibility for) any damnable actions committed by others because of a lack of evidence, even if they were personally involved or at least willfully ignorant of what was occurring, seems to have worked for many.

Over thirty suspects were arrested for the felony charge of cockfighting. To say the Cass County jail was on overload status that night is an understatement. To compound the issue, most of the suspects claimed to only speak Spanish, and not English. Later in the court process most had to be appointed attorneys, which only added to the costs the county was incurring.

Cockfighting suspects being led to transport van in Cass County after raid.
(Photo supplied from personal collection of anonymous photographer.)

In other words, this raid and subsequent bookings of over thirty suspects put a huge strain on the resources of Cass County, Nebraska.

The *Omaha World-Herald* ran several feature stories on this cockfighting raid. Matthew Hansen, a respected columnist, wrote a detailed article about how this incident was more than just birds fighting birds. It transcended so many other issues.

"The worst part may be that the 30 men and women now charged with felonies in Cass County are simply the tip of an awful iceberg," Hansen wrote.

I was interviewed by Hansen for this article. I told him, "I thought I would stop seeing bad people when I retired (from the Omaha Police Department)." I talked about how it was so much easier busting drug dealers in my early days than it was to learn about cockfighting in the Midwest.

"It's much more secretive than drug dealing. There's no loyalty in the drug world. There appears to be loyalty in this world," I told the reporter.

In another *World-Herald* article I talked of the scope of this cockfighting operation, and I called it "large and well organized."

I was also interviewed by a local TV station and made the famous statement (at least famous at the time to my coworkers): "We found razor blades tied to the cocks!"

I probably should have worded that better.

Lethal razor blade tied to foot of fighting cock.

Over thirty suspects, ranging in age from twenty-seven to sixty-two were arrested that night. All were later allowed to plead to reduced misdemeanor charges. Many were in this country illegally, and federal authorities were notified. We had suspects claiming to live in Nebraska as well as surrounding states and from Washington and California.

At least twenty to thirty suspects escaped the barn that night and were never located.

We received great cooperation from the Cass County Sheriff and the Cass County Attorney. I can't blame them for going with the reduced charges, working with the feds, and getting these guys out of their jail. In a perfect world I would have liked maximum prison sentences for all involved, but the criminal justice system is not perfect.

At least I would have liked to have seen the top organizers of this fight do some time. But we never determined who these people were since nobody talked.

Fighting bird seized from Cass County raid, 2018.

We held onto the 186 birds for several weeks until we received a judge's ruling that we could make humane decisions on their outcomes. The care of the birds was taxing on our staff. Most of the birds were nasty in nature, since being raised to bite and attack. We were able to adopt some of the birds to the community but, sadly, due to their aggressive personalities, most were humanely euthanized.

Though culturally accepted in Mexico, cockfighting is illegal in the United States. It is illegal for one specific reason: It's harmful and cruelly painful to the birds who are forced to fight to the death.

Remember Marvin Vogler, the owner of the property? Though he rented his barn to at least fifty participants for the cockfight event, and though he had over 180 birds in pens and cages throughout his property, Vogler maintained to me he had no knowledge of what was occurring. Instead, Vogler says a guy named "Walter" was the caretaker of the birds and came calling five to seven times a week to tend to the birds. Walter was never found.

Though Vogler continued his plausible deniability about the cockfighting taking place on his property, he told me he was worried that some of the guys arrested for fighting cocks might think he was the tipster that brought the operation down. He was genuinely concerned about his safety, along with his elderly mother whom he cared for in the house on the property.

A little over a week later, on December 6, 2018, Vogler's body was found in a field near his property. There was an empty pill bottle nearby, along with his phone. Investigators said the cause of death was from hypothermia associated with combined drugs in his system, including hydrocodone.

His death was ruled a suicide.

24

DOGFIGHTING UNTIL "THAT BITCH IS DEAD"

I t takes a detestable person to watch a dog viciously attacking another while, near death itself, the dog builds up one final surge of energy to clamp down on the opponent's throat, suffocating it to death.

It takes a shameful person to devote much of his life to buying, trading, and training dogs all for the main event, the champion bout, the pinnacle of a dogfighter's career.

It takes a deplorable person to take children to watch dogs pitted against each other in a fight to the death.

Early in my career at the Nebraska Humane Society I was given a video of a local dogfight in Omaha taking place in the dark dreary basement of a house. There was no fighting ring in place, which is normally found at organized, large-scale dogfights. Rather, there were simply two pit bull dogs owned by neighbors in the area set upon each other in an act of cruelty, all for the mighty buck being wagered by the twenty to thirty bettors yelling encouragement in the background.

The videographer was careful not to show the participants' faces. The pain and anguish of the two dogs forced to fight each other was apparent. The canines were consistently prodded to engage each other until the point was reached that each dog finally realized what they were meant to do.

The dogs cried in pain as they began tearing each other up. Blood was flying, and the excitement in the participants' voices began to escalate with each shriek of the dogs.

Suddenly in the video a small human voice is heard crying to his mom, obviously becoming traumatized by what his little eyes were being forced to watch.

"Mommy, I want to go home," the child said between tears, pleading for what every child in the world wants and needs—for his mother to protect him from bad, evil things.

Instead, Momma scolded the child to stop crying, yelling, "We're not going home until that bitch is dead!"

I have never forgotten that video, and though I was never able to verify who filmed it, where the fight happened, or who the organizers were, it provided me inspiration to go after the monsters who enjoy and promote the blood sport of dogfighting.

Believe me, I am aware of skeptics who feel there are worse crimes than dogfighting. Many times, I was asked why law enforcement should devote personnel and resources to animal crimes and instead switch the manpower and resources to people crimes.

I get it and agree wholeheartedly that trafficking kids for sex is way worse than dogfighting.

But I realized that dogfighting was not a stand-alone crime. Instead, it transcended so many other serious crimes involving gang activity, drug dealing, domestic violence, and child abuse.

To me, dogfighters were the definition of a violent criminal—and needed to pay the price.

INSIDE THE SECRET WORLD OF DOGFIGHTING

One early case I investigated at the Nebraska Humane Society involved a large and well-organized group of dogfighters based out of Omaha and the western part of Iowa.

The information came to me through the type of source I was well accustomed to utilizing during my days as a drug investigator with the Omaha Police Department.

A confidential informant contacted me and began laying out piece after piece of information about the locations where the dogfights were occurring, who the organizers were, and, most importantly, other crimes such as drug dealing that were associated with this criminal enterprise.

Confidential informants were my bread and butter during my time in the drug squad. These were individuals who told us details of crimes that we would not normally be privy to. Their motives for providing this information were varied.

The top three motives for informants I worked with over the years were (1) they wanted to get paid money for their information; (2) they were trying to work to gain leniency on crimes they were currently charged with; or (3) a scorned woman caught her drug-dealing boyfriend screwing around.

In order to protect this informant's identity, I am not going to divulge why he or she came forward on this dogfighting ring.

The information immediately struck me as being reliable. I also recall asking myself why I had not heard of these dogfighting activities up until now.

I learned, however, how secretive and cloistered the world of dogfighting is. I recognized the names of many of the suspects in the case. Some I had arrested for selling methamphetamine. Others I had received previous information on about their drug-dealing activities. Several names mentioned were previous informants of mine.

To say I was excited and intrigued about this particular informant coming forward is an understatement. The informant's information was clear. A group of culprits organized dogfights in barns in two counties in western Iowa. These acreages and farms were in rural areas, in order to minimize the chance of detection by law enforcement.

The fights were held every two to three months, with large crowds coming from all over the Midwest to attend. These were invitation-only events, with security at each site ensuring there were no uninvited guests. Wagering took place, as well as methamphetamine dealing and drug use. Guns were possessed by many in attendance, both for show and for personal protection in the event a dogfight (or drug deal) escalated into a human squabble.

The informant also shared that many pit bulls were being trained in clandestine locations throughout Omaha and western Iowa for these events.

Fighting dog impounded during 2009 raid in Johnson County, Nebraska.

My first step was a phone call to my former cohorts at the Omaha Police narcotics unit, who were immediately interested, based primarily on the methamphetamine-dealing angle. I was excited to again be working with some of my old crew and trying to nail another drug dealer.

The best police officers to help us on cases at the Nebraska Humane Society were animal lovers. I learned who these officers were, and I went straight to them when I needed help. A common conception of police officers is the hardened exterior they exhibit while showing no emotion. During my fifteen-year second career at the Nebraska Humane Society, I saw more than one cop tear up when we seized an emaciated puppy who was left in its kennel to starve. Would that same cop become emotional at a triple-homicide scene? In answering for myself, probably not.

AMAZING WHAT WE FOUND IN THE TRASH

We worked for months on this investigation. We located the main dogfighter's house in the North Omaha area. One night we went out late with undercover police officers and snuck down the dark alley behind the fighter's house. At the edge of the driveway were several bags of discarded trash, which we grabbed while hardly breaking stride.

Stealing people's trash is an investigative tactic that I used hundreds of times while a sergeant in the narcotics unit. The legal principle is this: If a suspect's trash is sitting in the normal pickup spot for the trash man, it's fair game to be seized by police officers.

One of the scariest parts of my job as an undercover police officer was trying to take people's trash. I felt like a thief, even though it was perfectly legal.

One time it was extremely late, and we covertly sauntered down a dark alley toward several trash bags lying at the edge of a driveway. We tried to be as quiet as possible, since if we were seen, the drug dealer would be alerted we were onto him, or worse, we might be mistaken for bad guys and get shot.

As I walked up to the trash bags, I heard this Darth Vader–type voice bellow, "Stay the fuck away from my trash!"

We ran like teenage kids who were caught trying to knock on a girl's window. We never saw the guy who yelled at us from his backyard and never went back there again.

It's amazing what drug dealers will discard in their trash. In fact, one of the worst parts of being a drug investigator is having to go through people's trash, especially during the hot summer months.

I recall going through discarded trash bags and finding plastic baggies with methamphetamine residue. Other valuable trinkets would be sheets of paper with drug records, names and phone numbers of other drug dealers, and packaging materials for what originally contained pounds and kilos of cocaine and methamphetamine.

But at the same time, we would be unwrapping paper tissues containing used condoms and tampons, which is why double-gloving was a requirement.

Low and behold, in this drug dealer/dogfighter's trash we found lots of methamphetamine residue, leading to a search warrant a few days later at his house. He wasn't home at that time, but we found evidence of both dogfighting and drug dealing.

We found a dealer amount of methamphetamine in a dresser drawer in his bedroom. Also in the same bedroom was a briefcase containing a huge amount of dogfighting parapher-nalia, including pictures of the dogs, names and phone numbers of other dogfighters, and a now-defunct dogfighting magazine called the *Sporting Dog Journal*.

The pictures in the briefcase depicted dogs being trained to fight through the use of a spring pole, suspended from a tree, with the pit bull latching its jaw onto the end and hanging above the ground for hours at a time. In the theory of dogfighters, this practice would strengthen the dog's jaw muscles, making for a better opponent in the ring.

*Polaroid photograph seized during 2005 dogfighting raid
shows a dog strengthening its jaws on a spring pole.*

Other pictures showed dogs being weighed for fighting purposes.

We found paperwork showing names of prominent dogfighters from southern states such as Louisiana and Tennessee, men well known to law enforcement in those regions. This told us there was a connection between the Omaha dogfighters to locations in the Southeast, which was the hot spot for dogfighting activities.

Sadly, we found no fighting dogs at his house.

But this search warrant exemplified to me the connection between dogfighting and drug dealing in the Nebraska-Iowa region.

A few months later, after more investigation, we hit another house accompanied by the Omaha Police Department's narcotics unit and members of the Emergency Response Unit (SWAT). This time we located a cache of weapons and more drugs.

But again, no pit bulls were located that were being fought. We later learned the dogs were hidden on a secluded acreage in Iowa.

We then assisted Iowa authorities in seizing about twenty dogs living on a quarter-acre lot secluded by a ten-foot-high ramshackle fence, which prevented the dogs from being seen from the country road nearby. There were also twenty blue barrels tipped on their sides, one for each dog, as shelter.

Fighting dogs hidden on an acreage in Iowa and seized in 2006.

Several months later the main dogfighter was federally indicated in Nebraska. He was charged with selling drugs, and not dogfighting. I was a bit disappointed in this. The federal prosecutors told me they had a better case on him for the drug dealing than for dogfighting.

During this investigation I was able to meet with several of the dogfighters who agreed to supply me information in exchange for not being criminally charged. Since I had no case against most of them to begin with, I agreed to do this to better understand the dogfighting world in Nebraska and Iowa. To some it may seem ridiculous to meet with a dogfighter and not arrest him. But these were guys who had a wealth of information that might be used later for those higher up in the food chain.

These men were like the many informants I had used while as a drug investigator. Only now, I was interviewing dogfighters in my role as the top cop at the Nebraska Humane Society.

I remember thinking to myself, "I simply cannot stay away from bad people."

Their interviews were a solid investigative tool, and I found the information both fascinating and useful in future dog-fighting investigations. Through these interviews I learned the dogfighting network in Omaha was much more organized and active than law enforcement ever realized.

In the early 1990s street fighting of dogs in Omaha began to become more prevalent. It is no small coincidence the timing matched the influx of gang members from California into Omaha. Crack cocaine dealing, drive-by shootings, and dogfighting began to escalate once the Bloods and Crips hit the streets of Omaha.

The bouts normally took place in basements or garages, consisting of gang members, wannabe gang members, neigh-borhood kids, older adults, and just about anybody who enjoyed betting a few bucks while watching two dogs, always pit bulls, tear themselves apart. Many times, the winner was declared when the other dog was too weak or injured to fight any further. At times, the dogs fought to the death, resulting in the corpse being dumped like a piece of trash.

This information coincided with dead pit bulls found by the Nebraska Humane Society in dumpsters, or in a city park near the Omaha airport, or dumped along the shoreline of a large lake. Most had evidence of dogfighting injuries. Others had bullet holes in the head, inflicted by the owners after the dog was deemed too weak for any more bouts.

Into the 2000s several of these street-level dogfighters became enamored with the sport (and I use that term lightly) and began escalating their activities into a more advanced stage. They began more regimented training for the dogs, utilizing the spring poles I mentioned, along with putting the dogs on treadmills for hours on end to build up their stamina.

Dark, secretive websites and chatrooms formed overnight in the late 1990s and early 2000s, allowing easy communication among local Omaha dogfighters and those nationally recognized as the elite. Suddenly, Omaha-area fighters were traveling to South Carolina, North Carolina, Louisiana, and Arkansas to buy fight dogs and to watch how top-level events were organized and conducted.

One of the dogfighters I talked to bragged of establishing an online relationship with a dogfighter from Ecuador, while arranging to have dogs shipped to Omaha for fighting purposes.

The name of an Iowa dogfighter came up prominently in my interviews. He lived in the country about sixty miles to the northwest of Des Moines and was considered an expert trainer and conditioner of dogs.

During these interviews I was both fascinated with the information being gleaned and concerned that I had never heard of this secretive and criminal network operating right under law enforcement's noses for years.

There were dogfighters in eastern Nebraska and western Iowa who owned twenty or thirty dogs housed mainly in the country on dilapidated acreages. The dogs existed on six-foot chains staked to the ground with access to round barrels tipped on their sides filled with straw or hay as insulation to stay warm in cold weather.

DOGS, METH, BETTING, AND GUNS

Dogfighting in the Omaha area really took off in the early 2000s. The big fighters were hosting large-scale fights every month or so. These events took place in different locations strewn throughout the countryside, both in Nebraska and Iowa. The fights were advertised both by word of mouth and on the internet. Only selected people were invited to participate, and unless you were in the know, it was hard to find out about them.

There were fighters designated as the promoters of these events. It was their job to secure a location, advertise the events, arrange for the bouts, and collect the required fees for all those in attendance.

Normally about fifty dogfighters and spectators would attend, with thousands of dollars being wagered. All the informants I interviewed told me there were common denominators at each of these events: dogs, dogfighters, wagers, methamphetamine, and guns.

Many times, these factors did not mix well. Fights among the human participants were common. Sadly, children were also a constant at these bloody events.

The dogfights normally took place in outbuildings or barns on the secluded properties, with a designated fight ring constructed in the middle. Normally the ring consisted of two-foot-high plywood sheets formed into a square big enough for all the participants to gather around.

Dogfighting ring seized from raid in North Omaha 2018.

There were actually referees who oversaw each individual bout. It was the promoter's job to have referees. These men were trained on recognizing when one dog had reached the point of defeat, like referees in boxing matches. Their word was golden, and arguing with their decisions was not allowed.

One of the dogfighters I interviewed offered an interesting insight into the world of dogfighting. According to him, many of the participants were white supremacists. It was common for Nazi war rallies to take place along with the dogfights. Armed sentries were posted around the perimeters of the properties to guard against law enforcement trying to conduct covert surveillance with night vision scopes.

During each bout there were handlers in the ring with the dog and the referee. It was the handler's job to make sure the dogs were actively engaged in fighting with each other. Many times, one dog was not as apt to participate as the other. The handlers would incite the dogs until both reached a point of frenzy. The handlers were also armed with break sticks, a long wooden stick used to pry the jaws of the pit bulls off each other to reengage the dogs to fight.

Most of the dogs involved in the organized fighting had severe injuries after the event. The point was not to fight to the death, as these dogs were a valuable commodity and were needed for future fights. But injuries such as broken bones and teeth, blood loss, shock, dehydration, exhaustion, or infections were severe and many times life-threatening.

However, the owners knew they could not take the dogs to a veterinarian for treatment since the vets would recognize the reasons for the injuries and in turn call law enforcement.

So these dogfighters trained themselves in street-level veterinarian care for their injured dogs. At times they sutured the dog's injuries with no anesthetic, a barbaric act which only added to the dog's agony.

Sometimes the dog's injuries were so severe that future fighting was not a reasonable expectation. In these cases, the most humane thing the owner did was to shoot the dogs in the head, putting them out of their misery. Many times, I was told the injured dogs were simply thrown to the side, dying a slow death while the next pair of dogs was thrown into the ring.

The professional dogfighter takes great pride in fighting their own dogs. They consistently train and condition their dogs with the use of anabolic steroids to enhance muscle mass and encourage aggressiveness. These "professionals" educate themselves about bloodlines of champion dogs and sell and buy dogs for thousands of dollars that meet the highest level of generational pedigree.

The professional dogfighter lives, eats, and breathes the world of dogfighting. Since he is also most likely a drug dealer, this man is also cognizant of informants trying to rat him out and law enforcement efforts to put him in jail.

Breeding is an important factor for a professional dogfighter. The use of rape stands is an abhorrent practice designed to use a device to physically hold a female dog while a male dog mounts her. They are used in cases where the female dog is too aggressive and/or unwilling to otherwise mate of her own volition.

I have taught seminars nationwide on dogfighting, after years of developing information about events in Nebraska and Iowa. I stress to the law enforcement personnel in attendance that dogfighting is not a stand-alone crime, and drugs and guns are a constant presence. Developing informants is difficult since dogfighting involves a dark, murky world of paranoid and cloistered individuals who do a good job of not transmitting their crimes.

Many dogfighting operations are busted by police officers simply stumbling onto them while investigating other crimes such as drug dealing, loud parties, and domestic disturbance calls. That's why it's important to train cops on the signs of dogfighting. The Nebraska Humane Society provides training on animal fighting and animal cruelty to police recruit classes so that the rookie officers know what to look for on the streets.

In Nebraska it is a felony not only to fight animals but to train them to fight and to sell them knowing they will be fought. Being a spectator at an animal fight is also a felony.

To bring light to animal fighting I decided to approach prospective donors about funding a reward fund just for animal fighting. It was an easy sell, and we broadcast to the public that the Nebraska Humane Society pays $10,000 for information leading to arrests for animal fighting.

Like tip lines for crime stoppers, we produced three short commercials for our local television stations stating: "Dogfighting is a felony, we pay cash for tips." "Watching a dogfight is a felony, we pay cash for tips." "Training a dog to fight is a felony, we pay cash for tips."

Nebraska Humane Society's animal control van
with message about dogfighting as a crime, 2019.

Each commercial displayed a blurred image of dogs fighting each other, with growling and snarling in the background. We took animal fighting seriously.

And though we had some successes, I know there are still organized dogfighting and cockfighting operations in these brutal blood sports taking place.

Now you know.

OVER AND OUT

I represent a small percentage of police officers who shot and killed a suspect in the line of duty. During that incident, I came close to losing a valued friend and fellow police officer. I tell that story in detail in my first book, *Busting Bad Guys*.

Now at age sixty, I realize how the twenty-six years I spent as a police officer formed me into the person I am today. There are some who might describe me as engaging, outgoing, and a leader. I tend to think of myself as brooding, suspicious, and reclusive. Depression creeps into this conversation, like how it slowly crept into my life.

How could it not have? Between my two careers over the past forty years, I have been exposed to the worst life can offer. Drug dealing, sex trafficking, murders, child abuse, and animal cruelty can take a toll.

Depression could easily win me over if I didn't have the fight to take it head on. Every day, I battle through self-preservation, family support, and psychological and medical help.

I stress to my fellow police officers who read this book around the country and the world that professional help is here for the taking. Though we think we are supermen and super-women, we are not. If you feel yourself sinking in quicksand, *make the call.*

Do not become a suicide statistic.

I also fight with the help of my loving wife, Annette, who inspires me daily with her infectious joy for life and positive attitude. She is a perfect example of how to love and support a cop during a challenging and dangerous career.

And she never complained. I love her forever.

My kids are my inspiration. Katie and Tommy have also chosen challenging and demanding careers in the areas of pharmacy and law. Both have already achieved greatness, and not just in their respective fields. Although no kids are perfect, I am proud to say that neither Katie nor Tommy caused us any headaches or heartaches while they were growing up. Both are great kids, and Annette and I are so proud of them.

And then there's Colin and Drew, two grandsons that we love to the moon and back. Annette and I decided early to totally devote ourselves to whatever these boys needed. Since then, sporting events, babysitting, overnighters, and what seems like hundreds of Happy Meals at McDonald's have reinvigorated us and given us a new purpose in life.

When both Colin and Drew are adults with kids of their own, I hope they read this when I say, "We loved you then, and we love you now!"

Thank you for giving Nana and Papa a new purpose in life.

Yes, I have seen a lot.

I have seen enough to write two books.

But I know that I have not yet seen it all.

I eagerly anticipate what is to come.

ACKNOWLEDGMENTS

This book took four years to research and compose. I enjoyed the writing process and have many to thank.

Retired Omaha Police Officers Randy Eddy and Greg Stanzel did a fantastic job reliving the events from 1988. Young police officers who read this book should view Randy and Greg as examples of the importance of teamwork while making a tough call in the most stressful of situations. Thanks to both of you for your service and for taking the time to sit down with me.

To Denise Rue, Laura Nalley, and Darla, the hostages of the 1988 siege, I say thank you. My intent was not to cause old scars to resurface. I wish you the best. You are true survivors.

Several of my confidential informants came forward to tell their harrowing life stories about the pitfalls of using methamphetamine, running with the Hells Angels, and being married to a drug-dealing husband with a woman hidden in your house. You are fascinating people and I am glad you chose me to tell your stories.

To "The Other Daughter." We have in common the idea of thinking of your father every day, though for different reasons. I wish you the best of luck.

Thank you to Joe Jeanette for sharing his views on the death penalty. I have known Joe for over thirty years. During our first case together, we took down the South Omaha drug organization run by "The Painter," which is vividly described in chapter 28 of my first book. Thanks for sticking to your convictions and for being a steady influence during all my careers.

A special thanks to Kelli Brown of the Nebraska Humane Society, whom I consider to be the best animal cop in the country. My heart aches for your recent loss, and I will always be a phone call or text away from you. Please promise to read your texts before you send them, because spell check can be a challenge.

To my editor Sandra Wendel who continues to challenge me in ways I need to be challenged. We share a love for true crime stories, and it shows in both of my books.

Lisa Pelto of Concierge Marketing in Omaha is one of my biggest supporters. Some of my best times in the past few years have been sharing a booth with you and selling lots of books. Let's keep it up with *More Busting Bad Guys*.

To my mother, Elizabeth Langan, who was one of the most street savvy people I knew. Nothing I did on the job surprised her. She loved hearing my war stories. Thank you for all you did for me, including giving up your apartment for a team of surveillance officers. I love and miss you every day. Katie and Tommy are doing great.

We lost my dear sister, Judi, since the publication of my first book. I miss her funny stories and the giggles that followed. We have a memorial garden in our backyard in her honor, and I look at it every day. You are missed, Judi.

My brother, Tom, is the youngest eighty-year-old around. You are an inspiration to me, and I am one of your biggest fans. I love you, big brother.

And finally, to my fellow police officers. I wrote this book as an opportunity to honor those who protect us. I think this is especially important when so many politicians, activists, and "musicians" seem willing to deride police officers as being less than honorable. Never forget, you have the support of the silent majority.

You will always have my support.

Blue will always be my favorite color.

ABOUT THE AUTHOR

Mark Langan served for twenty-six years with the Omaha Police Department. He worked in vice and undercover operations, notably as a narcotics sergeant in the narcotics unit. During his career Langan infiltrated high-level narcotics operations while posing as both a drug user and a drug dealer and supervised hundreds of high-risk investigations.

Langan wrote nationally published articles on various law enforcement topics and lectured throughout the country. Recognized as a court-authorized expert on narcotics investigations, he testified hundreds of times in both state and federal court.

He was awarded the department's two highest honors: the Distinguished Service Medal and the Medal of Valor.

After retiring from the Omaha Police Department, Langan spent fifteen years as the Vice President of Field Operations for the Nebraska Humane Society where he was responsible for the investigation of crimes involving animals. He continued writing articles for national law enforcement publications and was a recognized national speaker on animal cruelty and dogfighting issues.

In 2016 Langan's first book, *Busting Bad Guys: My True Crime Stories of Bookies, Drug Dealers, and Ladies of the Night,* was nationally recognized with a bronze IPPY award by the Independent Publisher Book Awards in true crime. That same year the book was also heralded by PoliceOne.com, a website dedicated to the professional development of police officers, as among the fifteen must-reads for police officers worldwide.

Mark Langan and his wife, Annette, live in Omaha where they spend time spoiling their grandkids.

READ THE FIRST BOOK IN THIS SERIES

"Nobody knows this crime territory better than Mark Langan. His authentic experience proves that he is an expert in telling a story worth listening to."
  —Alex Kava, *New York Times* Best-selling Thriller Author

Busting Bad Guys: My True Crime Stories of Bookies, Drug Dealers, and Ladies of the Night

Thirteen seconds of pure terror in a shootout with a drug dealer...

Real crime. Real-life cop stories.

Sergeant Mark Langan relives his front-row seat working the seamier side of crime during his decorated twenty-six-year career from youngest rookie in 1978 to narcotics sergeant on the Omaha Police force.

Langan caught bold burglars who silently entered homes to get thrills off of touching sleeping victims. He hit bookie joints in smoke-filled bars, squeezed snitches for information, and arrested prostitutes and their everyday "Johns" in dangerous downtown alleys.

Langan worked his way up the ranks to command under-cover narcotics operations in the 1980s when sinister LA gangbangers invaded Omaha and claimed neighborhoods to sell crack.

In his celebrated career, Langan felt the gut-wrenching pain of innocent children caught inside the wicked world of drugs and crime, their "safe" worlds shattered when the battering ram knocked down their doors—their cries haunt him every day. And two players from his past reemerge in startling ways.

Busting Bad Guys delivers a graphic and authentic look at solid policing on the streets of America's heartland and takes readers inside the high-adrenaline, top-secret investigations to develop innovative tactics to outsmart the criminals.

www.BustingBadGuys.com

Available on Amazon in paperback, ebook, and audiobook.